Solutions C

Solutions in C

Hundreds of Programming Tips by the Author of "Doctor C's Pointers"

Rex Jaeschke

Addison-Wesley Publishing Company, Inc.

Reading, Massachusetts · Menlo Park, California
Don Mills, Ontario · Wokingham, England · Amsterdam
Sydney · Singapore · Tokyo · Madrid · Bogota
Santiago · San Juan

Library of Congress Cataloging-in-Publication Data

Jaeschke, Rex.
  Solutions in C.

  Bibliography: p.
  Includes index.
  1. C (Computer program language) I. Title.
QA76.73.C15J34 1986   005.13'3   86–1042
ISBN 0–201–15042–5

Many of the designations used by manufacturers and sellers to distinguish their products are claimed as trademarks. Where those designations appear in this book, and Addison-Wesley was aware of a trademark claim, the designations have been printed in initial caps (for example, VisiCalc) or all caps (for example, UNIX).

Cover design by Marshall Henrichs
Text design by Carson Designs Inc.
Set in 10 point Century Schoolbook by Compset Inc., Beverly, MA.

ABCDEFGHIJ-HA-898765

First printing May, 1986

CONTENTS

PREFACE

C is the only language I have actually set out to learn. The other programming languages I know have been learned by osmosis under "battle" conditions: I was handed a language manual and a problem definition and asked to implement a solution yesterday. When these projects were completed, I knew enough about the language to know that either it was not the best language for the task or that my use of the language was, at best, inefficient. Consequently, the ability to maintain and modify these programs was significantly less than ideal.

Learning C was an entirely different matter. I decided to learn C; I didn't have any project deadline; I controlled my own hardware and system software environment and I was ready to learn from the mistakes I had made with other languages. From the outset, I decided to identify the classes of problems that C was best and least suited for. I evaluated C from a production programming manager's point of view and, in particular, I wanted to ascertain the cost of writing in C. This cost estimate was to include the requirements for training of C programmers, project management techniques, software development and debugging tools, and program maintenance.

During my three-year research period I found many answers, which then triggered many new questions. And each week I still find myself learning something new about the language or about the idiosyncrasies of one of its implementations. Perhaps the most significant impact on my efforts has been my involvement with the ANSI X3J11 C Language Standards Committee. If you think you know something about a language, try attending a five-day meeting with forty-five implementers of that language.

An often used quotation is that "To most people, all computers are the one they are currently using." Most of us work in a very narrow part of the world of computing, so we perceive the way something occurs or exists in our environment as the way it is in other environments. This clearly is not the case with C, due to its inherent relationship with the underlying hardware and system software. Therefore, if we confine ourself to C in one particular environment, we are denied the experience of seeing the many possible and legitimate flavors of C and of really appreciating its capabilities and pitfalls. Even when a language standard is released there will still not be just one C language.

During my research, I found an extreme shortage of material on such topics as pointers to functions, multi-dimensional arrays, the stack and heap, and program startup and termination. As a result, I spent many hours researching these topics with a number of different compilers on several different machine architectures. Needless to say, the end result was this book. As I felt that few people would have the same time, resources, and interest as I did to conduct research on C, I decided to make it publicly available, an effort which took almost as long as the research itself. My work has helped me significantly, to the point where I spend almost as much time trying to convince people not to use C as I do getting others to adopt it. If my work helps you at all, then we have both gained.

A number of people contributed to this book both directly and indirectly, so some thanks are in order: to Jim Brodie, Dennis Deloria, and Harry Foxwell, who provided valuable input to the manuscript. To Dennis Ritchie and Brian Kernighan for creating and promoting the C language so successfully. To P. J. Plauger for almost single-handedly starting the whole third-party C compiler industry. To my colleagues on the ANSI X3J11 C Language Standards Committee for providing me with much information and material for hours of contemplation, and to Jim Brodie for the foresight to actually form an ANSI Committee. Finally, to my wife, Jenny, who takes care of the vast majority of my domestic and business matters and thus allows me to spend inordinate amounts of time on my writing and research.

Rex Jaeschke

READER ASSUMPTIONS AND ADVICE

This book does not attempt to teach C. It is an advanced text. But if only the first three chapters deal with the more advanced capabilities of C as exist in a language definition, how is this an advanced book? The problems of finding an optimum program stack size and a reasonable header structure are indeed advanced, as are the important issues of program startup and termination. These issues go beyond learning the C language. They involve engineering a C project, which is much, much more than just writing code. The extensive coverage of these latter topics differentiate this book from other advanced C texts.

As with the proposed ANSI Standard, this book is written for users of both compilers and interpreters. The term *compiler* is used throughout to mean C program translator. Where a particular problem applies only to interpreters, that is so stated.

Small program examples in languages other than C are used in various places throughout the book. Such use is neither an endorsement for or against those languages. They are merely used to demonstrate the properties of languages other than C in addressing a given problem. The examples and languages have been chosen to help reinforce some particular capability, or lack thereof, in C. The languages chosen are very common, so that the majority of readers will likely be familiar with them.

Because the proposed ANSI Standard was not yet finalized at the time of writing, discussion of it is left to the end of each chapter except in Chapter 10 in which significant reference is made to the proposed run-time library part of the Standard. Appendices A and B contain considerable information about the Standard.

Some terminology has been borrowed from the proposed Standard. Examples are, *integral* (meaning any of the signed or unsigned integral types) and *implementation-defined* (assigned to behavior that is defined by a particular implementation). No new terminology has been introduced.

Several references are made throughout to `lint`, `make` and `grep`. These tools originated in the UNIX world and are now quite popular in other environments. `lint` is a tool that processes one or more C source code modules and reports on such things as intermodule argument calling discrepancies, the use of nonportable constructs, code that can never be reached, unused variables, and uninitialized pointers. `make` is a procedure by which a programmer can define a set of source modules and headers and their interrelationships. Then when any source module or header is modified, this procedure is invoked to compile all affected modules. `grep` (an acronym for General Regular Expression Parser) is a pattern matching utility that allows one or more text files to be searched for a given string.

INTRODUCTION

Every few years a new language appears on the horizon accompanied by disciples claiming it to be the ultimate programming tool. We have heard much about ALGOL, Pascal, C, Forth, and more recently, ADA, and sometimes it's been a case of "Much ado about nothing."

In this book some of the more advanced aspects of one of these "new" languages, C, will be discussed. However, before beginning, a few philosophical comments should help to put you in the proper frame of mind.

Right from the earliest days, natural languages were designed to describe the environment in which their speakers lived. Different isolated groups spoke different languages or dialects and literal translation from one language to the other was, and still is, oftentimes impossible. Likewise, computer languages have typically grown out of a narrow set of needs for one particular application or profession, and subsequently their vocabulary has been limited by that environment. For example, COBOL was designed for commercial applications, FORTRAN for engineering and scientific programming, and BASIC for teaching programming and problem-solving techniques.

While many languages are quite serviceable in areas outside their primary focus, none of them is everything to everybody. Indeed, if that were the case, we would all be using the same language and this book would not exist. The fact is that there has not been, nor is there likely to be, an ultimate language, and the sooner software design and programming professionals realize this the better.

C has been described as a midlevel or systems language. That is, it has many of the capabilities typically found only in assemblers, but it uses a high-level language vocabulary including such constructs as case, if/else, and do/while. C has been successfully used to implement operating systems (most notably UNIX), compilers (including most C compilers), interpreters, sort packages, and communication systems.

More recently, C has made significant inroads into commercial and applications programming, probably due to the widely touted portability claims and the increasing availability of good, cheap compilers and development libraries. While C can indeed be viewed as a high-level language, it should not be considered as a replacement for BASIC, FORTRAN, or COBOL. More likely it is replacing assembler and, in many cases, competes directly with Pascal.

This is not to say that good commercial programs can't be written in C. They can. If you have the ego and the time, most any program can be written in most any language, however, the real question is "Does it make sense?" No doubt there are many people currently implementing systems in C who just got caught up in the perceived state of the art and who may not be very successful in their efforts as a result.

We all have our favorite languages and during your involvement with C you probably have said at least once, "How primitive!" or "How complicated can you get? Language X is much better for that." If you don't like a particular aspect of C, just remember, no one promised that C was the ultimate language.

One of the most important things a programming manager can ever do is to pick the right language for the job at hand. Granted that available programming experience, time, and budget are important factors in this decision-making process, but using a particular compiler just because it's there is hardly good justification. And neither is the fact that C is supposedly state of the art. As Seymour Cray (the founder of Cray Research and prime architect of the Cray Supercomputers) once said, "The state of the art [for most people], is whatever they are doing now."

Bearing all this in mind, let's take a walk through the promised land of the language C.

Solutions in C

CHAPTER 1

Structures, Bit Fields, and Unions

STRUCTURES

Structures and File Records

Structures are excellent for handling variables in memory but they can present problems when dealing with data in files. There seems to be a high correlation between structures and disk file records, and it very much appears that they were meant for each other. However, on further inspection, this match may not be so harmonious. Consider the case of a disk file with records containing payroll information where a record's layout might be something like:

```
1234052384ROBERT E LEE 0567.89
```

The file was created by some other program (possibly written in a language other than C) and each record consists of six fields as follows.

1

Character Position	Field
1–4	Employee pay number
5–6	Payment month
7–8	Payment day
9–10	Payment year
11–30	Employee name
31–37	Amount of pay

The object of the exercise is to read a record from this file and store it in a structure of similar layout. If a command line of

```
program-name <input-file
```

is used where stdin is redirected to an input file (as allowed on UNIX, MS-DOS, and other systems), then the following program should suffice.

```
/* structl.c - read a record into a structure */

#include <stdio.h>

struct date {
    int month;
    int day;
    int year;
};

struct {
    int pay_num;
    struct date pdate;
    char name[21];
    float amount;
} st;
```

```
main()
{
    scanf("%4d %2d %2d %2d %20c %7f");
            &st.pay_num,&st.pdate.month,
            &st.pdate.day,&st.pdate.year,
            st.name,&st.amount);

    printf("pay number: %4d\n",st.pay_num);
    printf("pay date:    %02d/%02d/%02d\n",
            st.pdate.month,st.pdate.day,
            st.pdate.year);
    printf("emp name:    %s\n",st.name);
    printf("amount:      $%7.2f\n",st.amount);
}

pay number:  1234
pay date:    05/23/84
emp name:    ROBERT E LEE
amount:      $ 567.89
```

One problem with this program is the handling of the name field, because a name may contain embedded (and leading and trailing) white-space. If the name field were read using an edit mask of %20s, the scan would terminate at the first blank, that following the word "ROBERT". Then the scan for the float value would begin resulting in an error, as 'E' is not a valid floating-point value. (Note that for this particular data record, the 'E' may actually be interpreted as an exponent, resulting in a bogus float value being returned although a floating-point number usually must contain a decimal value or an exponent.)

The mask %20c gets around this limitation and causes 20 characters to be read. The mask %c causes the very next character to be read; white-space is not skipped. Normally, the value being read using a %c mask would be a character and therefore its address must be given to scanf. However, with %20c a character array is being read and the array name causes the address of that array to be passed to scanf. Of course, &name[0] could have been used instead of name.

While this technique allows a input string containing white-space, it leads to several problems. When the %s mask is used, scanf automatically adds the trailing '\0'. The %20c mask does not. As it happens, name[20] was initialized with a value of '\0' (by default) as it is an external variable, so when it is displayed using printf("...%s...") everything works properly. However, if name had been an automatic array, the terminating '\0' would have to be added explicitly.

The other problem is that %s causes the trailing '\0' to be added immediately after the last non-white-space character, whereas %20c reads in and keeps all trailing white-space. In the latter case, strlen(name) would always be 20, regardless of the text contained in the name field. If the trailing spaces are a problem, they will have to be removed by a user-written function.

The above method works reasonably well for formatted input, but unformatted data is quite another matter. Since many data files contain both text and binary data, it becomes necessary to write custom routines to read and write these records. Of course, binary fields could be read as characters or character arrays and then be rearranged (with byte and word swapping, etc.) to reconstruct the value actually represented, but this is very messy and error prone.

One possible solution is to read and write a whole structure rather than dealing with a field at a time, and that leads us to a discussion of internal structure layouts. (This can be done with the fread and fwrite library routines, but it may result in structure alignment holes being included in the file. If a record contains strings, they must be terminated with a '\0' if they are to be read and stored properly by fread.)

Structure Alignment

The C language makes no statement whatsoever concerning the alignment of structures. There are no rules about whether structures begin on specific boundaries, so these details are left to the compiler implementer. On machines such as the DEC PDP-11, integral and floating-point variables (and usually all pointers) may only start at word or longword boundaries and this may lead to holes in structures containing variables of these types. (Note that even on machines that do not require such alignment, like the DEC VAX-11 and the Intel 8086, certain performance improvements can be obtained by aligning on word or longword boundaries as this reduces the number of bus and/or memory cycles needed to address and transfer these quantities.)

Is all this important, and if so, why? Consider a machine such as the PDP-11, which requires everything except characters to be word aligned, on which exists the following fragment of code.

```
/* struct2.c - structure alignment example */

struct st {
    char c;
    int i;
    char d;
};

struct st st1, st2;
```

Like most C programmers you have probably assumed, with good reason, that multiple instances of the same structure have exactly the same amount of storage space allocated (at least within the same compiler), but the C language does not actually guarantee that. Compiler writers have to align structures on some kind of boundary so that arrays of structures can be defined and accessed correctly.

The space allocated to a structure can be determined by using the `sizeof` operator as follows.

```
/* struct3.c - sizeof and structures */

struct test {
    char c;
    int i;
    char d;
    float f;
};

struct test t1, t2;
```

The value `sizeof(t1)` is the same as `sizeof(t2)`, which is also the same as `sizeof(struct test)`. This means that alignment considerations are taken into account when the structure is declared and *not* when specific instances of it are defined. Array element references are usually dealt with as pointers and offsets so, in an array of structures, members must begin at the same offset within each element and holes in any one element must exist at exactly the same offset in all elements. (For this reason, structures must also end on the same kind of boundary that they started on.)

Back to the Problem

If you want to read and write complete structures to and from files, you must understand how structures are stored. Consider the following structure, where objects in memory are to be stored in disk file records and later read back.

```
/* struct4.c - I/O structure */

struct io {
    int i;
    char c[20];
    float f;
} stru;
```

Assuming a binary output function called writstru exists, a record can be written using

```
writstru(file, stru, sizeof(stru));
```

The complete structure stru is written out, starting with the first byte. (Note that sizeof should be used rather than an explicit length.) The int and float values are written out as binary bytes and the whole char array c is written, including the trailing '\0' (if c is a string). The reverse process can be used to retrieve the record. If the record were written by a program created with one C compiler and read in with a program created on a different compiler, it is possible that the compilers' structure alignment for the same structure may be different in which case the record read back would not correspond exactly with that written out.

Reading and writing records from the same (or similar) programs is not a problem, but in the very first example, the file was created by some other means. Perhaps the best method of reading formatted records is that shown

0703 59° 2,53

with `scanf`, although trailing spaces at the end of strings will need to be removed. Binary data can easily be handled by reading the record into a structure, provided the external fields are aligned appropriately. Reading text fields into a structure with a binary read is a real problem, unless those fields already contain a trailing `'\0'`. A name field on disk may be 20 characters long, but 21 are required in a structure if the string is to be used properly within the program; this would prohibit the record from being read as a whole. Strings have to be input by field.

Copying and Comparing Structures

It is quite likely that once you begin using structures, you will want to make copies of them for later restoration or comparison.

```
struct s1 {
    char c;
    int i;
};

struct s1 sa, sb;

struct s2 {
    char c;
    int i;
};

struct s2 sc;
```

The structures sa and sb have the same size and type so they can safely be copied to one another, but what about sa (or sb) and sc? Since the member type and order of these structures are identical, the structures have the same size so sa and sb should be able to be copied to and from sc. (Note that this is not guaranteed by the language, because strictly speaking, the structures s1 and s2 are considered to be different data types.) The problem now remains to perform the copy. The library function `strncpy(sb,sa,sizeof(sa))` may work in many cases but this is a string copy routine. If any binary field contains a zero byte (or a `'\0'` terminated string is present), the copy is terminated prematurely.

```
/* struct5.c - copying structures by bytes */

struccpy(dest,source,length)
char *dest, *source;
int length;
{
    if (length <= 0)
            return;

    while (length--)
            *dest++ = *source++;
}
```

This function copies a whole structure without regard to its contents. However, it assumes char pointers as its first two arguments when in fact they will never be passed that way. Although the vast majority of C implementations use the same amount of storage for all pointer types, this is not always the case, so struccpy should be invoked using something like

---

```
struccpy((char *)sb, (char *)sa, sizeof(sa))
```

By using explicit casts, compilers or *lint*-like checkers will not complain of argument type mismatch.

If you do a lot of structure copying, or copy very large structures, you may try to cut corners by moving machine words instead of bytes, as follows.

```
/* struct6.c - copying structures by words */

struccpy(dest,source,length)
int *dest, *source;
int length;
{
    if ((length /= 2) <= 0)
            return;
```

8

```
      while (length − −)
            *dest++ = *source++;
}
```

This version is inherently nonportable as it assumes a word is two bytes long. The pointers should be cast to pointers to `int`, when `struccpy` is called. The same idea may be extended to copying by long machine words provided the size of the structure is guaranteed to be an integral multiple of `sizeof(long)`.

Comparing two structures can be as difficult as copying them. Consider two structures which because of alignment constraints have holes in them. If they are automatic structures, these holes will contain unpredictable data. (Note that all members in `static` and external structures are guaranteed to be initialized to zero. Structures stored in dynamic memory allocated by `calloc` have each member initialized to "all bits zero" which may not be the same as a member with a value of zero, particularly in the case of floating-point variables.) Even if two structures have identical member values, their hole values may differ, in which case a byte-by-byte comparison similar to the byte/word copy functions above may not work. The only predictable way to compare structures is by comparing each and every one of their members separately.

Alignment Revisited

The above discussion of structure internal layouts may be more than most programmers need, but common sense dictates that they should at least recognize a good and bad structure layout and whether such a thing can exist on their systems. The following example shows three different ways to define the same structure. Some of these layouts are better than others, although all of them will work just fine.

```
/* alternate structure organizations */

#include <stdio.h>

struct {
    char c1;
    int i1;
    char c2;
    char *pc;
    char c3;
    float f1;
} st1;

struct {
    char c1;
    char c2;
    char c3;
    int i1;
    char *pc;
    float f1;
} st2;

struct {
    float f1;
    char *pc;
    int i1;
    char c1;
    char c2;
    char c3;
} st3;

main()
{
    printf("st1 = %d bytes\n",sizeof(st1));
    printf("st2 = %d bytes\n",sizeof(st2));
    printf("st3 = %d bytes\n",sizeof(st3));
}
```

The results of the above program will be implementation-defined and may vary from 11 to 18 bytes or more. While the compiler controls the actual member alignment (if any), by some simple reordering of the members it may be possible to cause a structure to be more densely packed, thus taking up less storage space. Assuming that all types other than char must have int alignment, structure st1 is the worst possible organization as byte and word aligned members are alternated and a byte (3 bytes on a VAX) will be wasted after each char member. Structure st2 is better than st1 but not as good as st3, which makes the best use of member packing. Structures are typically aligned on the most stringent boundary requirement of any of the contained members, in which case by ordering members in descending order of alignment requirements, the best usage of space can be obtained.

One subtle note is that pc is a pointer to a char, it is *not* a char itself. On DEC machines pointers are typically implemented as words or longwords, and therefore they will be subject to the same alignment constraints (and benefits) as those object types.

It is possible (perhaps probable) that a compiler will force all structures in a program to have exactly the same alignment regardless of the member types they contain. The following program will provide the minimum structure allocation requirement for your compiler.

```
/* struct7.c - find minimum structure size */

#include <stdio.h>

struct {
    char c;
} st;

main()
{
    printf("sizeof(st) = %d\n",sizeof(st));
}
```

If a compiler forces double or long int alignment on all structures, considerable space may be wasted, particularly if arrays of structures are used.

Archaic Member Referencing

There are several alternate ways to reference members via pointers to structures. While they are perfectly legal, their usage is rare.

```
/* struct8.c — alternate member access */

struct xx {
    int i;
    /* ... */
} st;

main()
{
    struct xx *pst = &st;
    int j;

    j = pst->i;      /* common method */
    j = (*pst).i;    /* rarely used */
    j = (&st)->i;    /*    "        " */
}
```

Structures and Absolute Addresses

K&R states that in x->y x may be either a pointer to a structure (or union) *or* an absolute machine address. On the PDP-11, the I/O page is mapped into physical memory so that device registers look just like regular memory to any task that can map to this area. To access these device registers, use something like:

```
/* struct9.c — structures and absolute
                addresses. */

#include <stdio.h>
```

```
#define IOPAGE 0xFF000
#define DEVICE1 0xFF000
#define DEVICE2 0xFF010

struct devreg {
    unsigned int status;
    unsigned int vector;
};

main()
{
    printf("Device 1 register status = %u\n",
            DEVICE1->status);

    DEVICE2->status = 0xABCD;
}
```

Not all compilers allow this type of member reference and compilers having a different member name-space for each structure will reject the above program because of possible ambiguous member references, as follows.

```
/* struct10.c - absolute addresses confusion. */

#include <stdio.h>

#define IOPAGE 0xFF000
#define DEVICE1 0xFF000
#define DEVICE2 0xFF010

struct devreg1 {
    unsigned int status;
    unsigned int vector;
};

struct devreg2 {
    int i;
    unsigned int status;
};

main()
{
    printf("Device 1 register status = %u\n",
            DEVICE1->status);

    DEVICE2->status = 0xABCD;
}
```

In this instance of x–>y x is an absolute value, *not* a structure pointer, so the compiler can't qualify the member named status by a structure pointer. The compiler has no way of knowing which status member is being referred to, and as each has a different offset within its structure, the reference is ambiguous.

The solution is to cast the absolute address to a pointer to the appropriate structure type. In struct10.c, this requires

---

```
((struct devreg1 *)DEVICE2)->status = 0xABCD;

instead of:

DEVICE2->status = 0xABCD;
```

Likewise, the reference to DEVICE1->status also needs to be changed.

Miscellaneous Comments

There are occasions where a member may be legitimately referenced by
something like x.y->z.

```
/* struct11.c - mixing "." and "->" */

#include <stdio.h>

struct dummy1 {
    char c;
    int i;
} ds1;

struct dummy2 {
    float f;
    struct dummy1 *pds1;
} ds2;

main()
{
    ds2.pds1 = &ds1;
    ds2.pds1->i = 5;

    printf("ds1.i = %d\n",ds1.i);
}


ds1.i = 5
```

15

This occurs with self-referential structures (or unions) and with structures containing members that point to other structures (or unions).

All members within a structure (except bit fields) must be named. There can be no explicit filler as in COBOL where a group item may contain one or more occurrences of FILLER. (FILLER in COBOL is typically used to provide spacing when constructing printed reports or display screens and to skip unwanted fields on record input.)

Consider the following structure definition.

```
/* struct12.c — structures and instances */

static struct ss {
    char c;
    int i;
};

struct ss ss1;
```

The structure definition is perfectly legal, but the storage class `static` is ignored. To the reader, it may imply that all instances of that structure will be created as `static`, but this is not the case. The storage class of a structure is that specified when space is allocated to an instance of a structure, not when the structure is declared.

The X3J11 Draft

The proposed draft Standard contains the following comments about structures.

- There may be unnamed holes within a structure, but they cannot occur at the beginning.

- Each structure has a separate name-space. The same member name can exist in multiple structures without conflict. (K&R allowed this provided certain offset considerations were obeyed. The K&R approach was enforced in UNIX Version 7–era compilers and is still implemented by a number of popular compilers.)

16

- Structures can be assigned using `s1` = `s2` provided that both the structures `s1` and `s2` are of the same type. This capability supplants the earlier discussion on structure copying, but until your compiler supports this capability, you will still have to deal with the problem. (Refer to example `union12.c` below for an example of union assignment that is similar to structure assignment.)

- Structures may be passed to functions as arguments and returned as function return values. This will break existing code that doesn't use `&structure` when passing a structure pointer. In future, the & operator will be necessary when passing structure pointers. (Refer to example `union13.c` below for an example of passing unions by value and address. This is very similar to passing structures by value and address.)

BIT FIELDS

A bit field is a special type of structure member in that several bit fields can be packed into an `int`. While bit fields are variables, they are defined in terms of bits rather than `chars` or `ints`. Bit fields are useful for maintaining single or multiple bit flags in an `int` without having to use logical AND and OR operations to set and clear them. They can also assist with constructing and dissecting bytes and words that are sent to and received from external devices.

Introduction

Before going on to more advanced bit-field techniques, some elementary bit-field definition and usage discussion is in order.

```
/* fieldl.c - introduction to bit fields */

#include <stdio.h>

struct bitfield {
    unsigned fl : 1;
    unsigned f2 : 2;
    unsigned    : 3; /* 3 bit filler */
    unsigned f4 : 4;
    unsigned f5 : 5;
    unsigned f6 : 6;
    unsigned    : 0; /* force int alignment */
    unsigned f8 : 8;
};

struct bitfield bf;        /* define structure */

main()
{
    bf.fl = 1;         /* stores 1 in 1 bit */
    bf.f2 = 0x3;       /* stores 3 in 2 bits */
    bf.f4 = 0xff;      /* truncate, store 15 in 4 bits */
    bf.f5 = -4;        /* truncate, store 28 in 5 bits */
    bf.f6 = 0377;      /* truncate, store 63 in 6 bits */

    /* f8 is not initialized explicitly */

    printf("bf.fl is %u\n",bf.fl);
    printf("bf.f2 is %u\n",bf.f2);
    printf("bf.f4 is %u\n",bf.f4);
    printf("bf.f5 is %u\n",bf.f5);
    printf("bf.f6 is %u\n",bf.f6);
    printf("bf.f8 is %u\n",bf.f8);
}


bf.fl = 1
bf.f2 = 3
bf.f4 = 15
bf.f5 = 28
bf.f6 = 63
bf.f8 = 0
```

A bit-field definition looks much like that for any other structure member with two exceptions. First, bit fields are typically unsigned quantities (although `int` or `signed int` bit fields may be supported by some newer compilers). Signed bit fields are not commonly implemented, but they can be useful in applications that need to deal with large numbers of small, signed values. Second, a colon separator is present. (While a colon also terminates a `goto` label definition, its use in structures is clear.)

The bit fields of length 3 and 0 in the above example are used for filler and `int` alignment respectively. The idea of an unnamed filler bit field is useful when dealing with external I/O ports and status words, etc. It allows you to make room for one or more bit fields without having to name them. If they don't have names, they cannot be accidentally used or overwritten. Of course, if they aren't named, you can't directly reference them, and playing tricks to get at them via the address of their parent `int` is dangerous. If your compiler doesn't support unnamed bit fields, give them a meaningless and obvious dummy name. The unnamed field of length of zero, above, forces the next field to have `int` alignment.

Storage Order

Depending on the underlying hardware, bit fields may be packed into machine words left to right or right to left. Different compilers for the same system may also having different packing methods. (A compiler may accept bit field definitions storing them each as `int`s which is certainly a problem when dealing with external data.)

If you are maintaining internal tables of flags without regard to externally imposed formats, the ordering of bit fields is not important. In this case, the convenience factor justifies their use. However, if you are picking apart or constructing bytes or words to go to and from the outside world, you will obviously need to control the exact bit ordering. If your compiler generates assembly code, that will give you the ordering it uses, although something like the following program should suffice.

```
/* field2.c - variable redefinition */

#include <stdio.h>

struct nibble {
    unsigned nibble1 : 4;
    unsigned nibble2 : 4;
    unsigned nibble3 : 4;
    unsigned nibble4 : 4;
};

union bitfield {
    struct nibble n;
    int i;
} u;

main()
{
    u.i = 0;

    u.n.nibble1 = 1;
    u.n.nibble2 = 2;
    u.n.nibble3 = 3;
    u.n.nibble4 = 4;

    printf("u.i = %x\n",u.i);
}


u.i = 1234        /* one possible outcome */

u.i = 4321        /* another possible outcome */
```

Here, four 4-bit bit fields have been initialized and redefined as an int. (This example was run on a 16-bit machine.) Two different compilers on the same system gave different results as shown. One packed bit fields left to right and the other right to left. (You may also wish to consider the byte ordering within words and word order within longwords.)

While programmers may not be interested in how bit fields are packed, there are some obvious orderings to avoid when defining them. Bit fields are

20

packed as they are encountered in the structure. The compiler *cannot* optimize storage by reordering them. So the order of their definition can be very important if you are concerned about storage.

```
/* field3.c - multiple declarations and ordering */

#include <stdio.h>

struct recordl {
    int il;
    unsigned ubla : 2, ublb : 4, ublc : 5;
    char cal[10];
};

struct record2 {
    unsigned ub2a : 2;
    int i2;
    unsigned ub2b : 4;
    char ca2[10];
    unsigned ub2c : 5;
};

main()
{
    printf("sizeof(recordl) = %2d\n",
            sizeof(struct recordl));
    printf("sizeof(record2) = %2d\n",
            sizeof(struct record2));
}


sizeof(recordl) = 14
sizeof(record2) = 18
```

Structure recordl is obviously a better approach than record2, as recordl takes full advantage of bit-field packing whereas record2 gives the worst possible case. Note that multiple bit fields can be defined in the same statement just as for "regular" variables.

Restrictions

You may be tempted to try to get the size or the address of bit fields as follows.

```
/* field4.c - sizeof and address-of operators */

#include <stdio.h>

struct bitfield {
   unsigned bf1 : 3, bf2 : 5;
} st;

main()
{
   printf("sizeof(st.bf1) = %u\n",sizeof(st.bf1));
   printf("addr of st.bf2 = %u\n",&(st.bf2));
}
```

Bit fields cannot be used with the sizeof operator. However, as the compiler allocated space in a structure for a bit field, it really does know how big it is, at least in terms of bits. The problem arises in that sizeof returns a size in bytes, not bits, and consequently this operation is illegal. Compilers that do accept this operator typically return the size of the object in which the named bit field has been packed (e.g. an int of 2 or 4 bytes).

Most machines cannot directly address bits. They are typically byte- or word-addressable only so the concept of "address of a bit field" makes no sense. Again, compilers that try to implement &bit field return the address of the parent int.

If you really need to use a bit field's size elsewhere in a program, it can be defined using a compile-time macro as follows.

```
/* field5.c - using macro width definitions */

#include <stdio.h>
```

22

```
#define BF1SIZE 3
#define BF2SIZE 5

struct bitfield {
    unsigned f1 : BF1SIZE;
    unsigned f2 : BF2SIZE;
} bf;

main()
{
    bf.f1 = 7;
    bf.f2 = 16;

    printf("bf.f1 = %2d\n",bf.f1);
    printf("bf.f2 = %2d\n",bf.f2);
}
```

The preprocessor only does string substitution, so by the time the compiler gets the actual bit-field definition, the syntax is valid. And of course, the compile-time constants BF1SIZE and BF2SIZE can be used anywhere throughout the program.

Some compilers may not permit bit fields to be the same size as an int. In this case, bit fields may only be 1 to 15 bits long on a 16-bit machine. Presumably, you should be using an int (or short) variable anyway.

Since bit fields are variables it might be useful to have arrays of them, but this is not allowed. The problem in implementing arrays of bit fields is that word-boundary considerations may require unused bits between logically adjacent bit fields, in which case there is no way to guarantee that elements within a bit-field array would have a calculable offset from the start of the array.

Bit fields are not permitted in unions. However, they can be defined in a structure that is itself part of a union. (Note that X3J11 changes this.)

There is perhaps a more obscure problem that arises when dealing with bit fields in nested structures. Consider the case where a number of bit fields can naturally be broken into a hierarchy of bit fields. For example, an operating system file protection scheme has 16 single-bit bit fields packed into a word. Each disk file has a protection word and each user access attempt is verified by checking the appropriate bits in this word. Assuming there are four classes of users and within each class, there are four file access modes, so the sixteen 1-bit fields naturally fall into four groups of four 1-bit bit fields. The problem is, how to declare such a structure. (This file protection mechanism is used by DEC's VAX/VMS and RSX-11 operating system families.)

```
/* field6.c - "erroneous" struct definition */

struct mode {
   unsigned read   : 1;    /* read access */
   unsigned write  : 1;    /* write access */
   unsigned extend : 1;    /* extend access */
   unsigned delete : 1;    /* delete access */
};

struct mask {              /* classes */
   struct mode system;
   struct mode owner;
   struct mode group;
   struct mode world;
};

struct mask promask;       /* define structure */
```

One structure has been declared to contain the four 1-bit access-mode bit fields and another structure contains four instances of the first structure. This idea is perfectly legal, makes the definition and code usage more obvious, and will run without error. However, it will *not* give the expected result.

On a 16-bit machine the four 1-bit bit fields in the structure mode are indeed packed into an int just as you would expect. The problem comes with the structure mask. This structure contains four other structures, all of the same layout, 4 bits. Structures are always aligned on certain boundaries as selected by the compiler writer, and while these requirements may vary, structures can never begin on bit boundaries. For the above example to work, the four structures system, owner, group, and world would have to be packed into the same int word, and this is not possible.

Perhaps the following example will clarify the problem.

```
/* using the structures declared above */

#include <stdio.h>

main()
{
    printf("Size of struct mode = %d bytes\n",
            sizeof(struct mode));
    printf("Size of struct mask = %d bytes\n",
            sizeof(struct mask));
}


Size of struct mode = 2 bytes
Size of struct mask = 8 bytes
```

These values are taken from a PDP-11 example where an int is 16 bits (2 bytes). The key is the size of struct mask, which contains the 4 other structures. It is 8 bytes (or 4 ints) and implies that each of the structures contained within take up their own word. That is, the four 4x1-bit bit fields are packed into four different words rather than into the same one. And this is not what we want. The correct solution to this problem requires each of the sixteen 1-bit bit fields to be defined in the same structure.

Initialization

Initialization and assignment for bit fields is just like that for other variables.

```c
/* field7.c - bit field initialization */

#include <stdio.h>

struct bitfield {
    int i;
    unsigned f1 : 5;
    unsigned f2 : 9;
    double d;
};

struct bitfield bf = {12345,27,500,3.456};

main()
{
    printf(" bf.i = %5d\n",bf.i);
    printf("bf.f1 = %5u\n",bf.f1);
    printf("bf.f2 = %5u\n",bf.f2);
    printf(" bf.d = %8.2f\n",bf.d);
}


bf.i = 12345
  bf.f1 = 27
 bf.f2 = 500
    bf.d = 3.46
```

Unions of Bit Fields

Redefining an int or char as a number of bit fields can be useful. The same approach can be taken in remapping one set of bit fields with another, as follows.

```
/* field8.c - unions of bit fields */

#include <stdio.h>

struct bfieldl {
    unsigned value : 4;
};

struct bfield2 {
    unsigned vbitl : 1;
    unsigned vbit2 : 1;
    unsigned vbit3 : 1;
    unsigned vbit4 : 1;
};

union bitfield {
    struct bfieldl bfl;
    struct bfield2 bf2;
} u;

main()
{
    u.bfl.value = 10;
    printf("u.bf2.vbitl = %u\n",u.bf2.vbitl);
    printf("u.bf2.vbit2 = %u\n",u.bf2.vbit2);
    printf("u.bf2.vbit3 = %u\n",u.bf2.vbit3);
    printf("u.bf2.vbit4 = %u\n",u.bf2.vbit4);
}
```

Code Generation

The ability to deal with bit fields as variables is very attractive as it lets programmers deal with logical rather than physical concepts and it relieves them from the tedious task of bit shifting and masking. However, if you do a lot of manipulation of bit fields, you will no doubt be interested in how efficiently this is being done.

Many modern architectures provide a reasonable set of bit manipulation instructions, but generic compilers (those that are ported among machines without necessarily being efficient on any of them) may not take proper advantage of these instructions. If you are really concerned about this, you may wish to revert to doing your own packing and unpacking. Apart from the instruction set, some compilers generate downright dreadful code anyway, and since bit fields are not overly used, this part of the compiler may not be tested as much.

If speed is a factor, then making each bit field an `int` instead may help considerably. This will eliminate the shifting and bit masking operations at the expense of increased storage (and the inability to deal with externally supplied bit-encoded data).

Conclusion

While bit fields may seem like a very good idea, and they are, there seem to be considerable differences in the way they are being implemented. If you are accessing control bytes or words supplied by your operating system or from some external source, you should look at the generated code for your compiler to see how it allocates storage for bit fields. Even if their ordering is not critical, a look at the order imposed may help in their understanding.

The X3J11 Draft

A number of things have been clarified in the proposed draft Standard. They are:

- A bit field's width must be an integral expression with a nonnegative value.

- Bit fields may be of type `int`, `unsigned int`, or `signed int`.

- A bit field cannot exceed the size of an `int`; that is, it can be less than or equal in size.

- Unnamed bit field declarations include a colon and width only. This means that the type as well as the name, must be absent.

- A bit field may be a member of a union without first having to be part of a structure.

- The size of the holding unit into which bit fields are packed, is implementation-defined.

UNIONS

The idea of a multipurpose variable storage area is not new to high-level languages — FORTRAN's EQUIVALENCE statement permits data areas to be redefined as does COBOL's REDEFINES clause. C provides a similar capability in the union. Not only are unions easy to define but arrays of unions are also easy to implement and use, as are pointers to unions. While structures and unions have some basic operational differences, they are defined and manipulated in a similar fashion. Therefore, in learning about one of these two aggregates you also learn a lot about the other.

A Practical Use

Applications often have to deal with a number of different input transaction types, where each input record has a different field layout except for a common record type field. Records may be variable or fixed length. Because only one input record can be processed at a time, space must be reserved for just that record, and if an input record's length depends on its record type, space must be allocated for the largest possible length.

One key aspect of this problem is that the record type of the input record is not known until the record has been read. Only when the type is known do we know which record definition to use to interpret the remainder of the data.

```
/* union1.c — handling multiple record types. */

#include <stdio.h>

struct rectype1 {
    int rectype;
    int var1a;
    long var1b;
    float var1c;
};

struct rectype2 {
    int rectype;
    float var2a;
    int var2b;
};

struct rectype3 {
    int rectype;
    float var3a;
    long var3b;
    int var3c;
};

union record {
    struct rectype1 rt1;
    struct rectype2 rt2;
    struct rectype3 rt3;
};

main()
{
    union record inrec;

    /* fake a getrecord(inrec) */

    inrec.rt1.rectype = 5;

    switch (inrec.rt1.rectype) {

    case '1' :
            /* ... */
            break;
```

```
        case '2' :
                /* ... */
                break;

        case '3' :
                /* ... */
                break;

bad:            default :
                printf("Record type %d received.\n",
                        inrec.rt1.rectype);
                break;
        }
        printf("inrec.rt1.rectype = %d\n",
                inrec.rt1.rectype);
        printf("inrec.rt2.rectype = %d\n",
                inrec.rt2.rectype);
        printf("inrec.rt3.rectype = %d\n",
                inrec.rt3.rectype);
}


Record type 5 received.
inrec.rt1.rectype = 5
inrec.rt2.rectype = 5
inrec.rt3.rectype = 5
```

The union `inrec` is big enough to hold a record of either type 1, 2, or 3. Each record type's layout is defined with a different structure and all such structures are contained within a union. Because all members of a union begin at offset zero, each of the three record definitions begins at the same address within the union.

If a union contains a number of structures, each of which has a common initial member sequence and the union currently contains data stored according to any one of these structures, then the common initial part of *any* of these structures can be reliably used. In all other cases, the results of interpreting the contents of a union via one structure when the data was stored via another structure, are implementation-defined. Each of the three record types has a common initial member sequence — they all have a variable called `rectype` as their first member. Therefore, when a record of any type is input, the type of that record can be checked using either `inrec.rt1.rectype`, `inrec.rt2.rectype`, or `inrec.rt3.rectype`.

All three members refer to exactly the same storage area within the union as demonstrated by the example above.

This example seems to be very straightforward, but does this mean that the record type must be the first field in each record? For the construct to be portable, all fields common to each record type must appear at the start of the structure definitions so that any alignment requirements can be satisfied. While the record type field usually is the first field, it could appear anywhere in the common fields. Of course, if the record type is the only common field, it must be the first.

Pointers to Unions

Just as structures can be passed by address, so too can unions. The following program illustrates a problem that may occur when actual and formal function arguments do not match.

```
/* union2.c - pointers to unions as arguments. */

#include <stdio.h>

/* use rectypex definitions from above */

union record {
    struct rectypel rtl;
    struct rectype2 rt2;
    struct rectype3 rt3;
} u;

main()
{
    printf("size of rtl = %d\n",sizeof(u.rtl));
    printf("size of rt2 = %d\n",sizeof(u.rt2));
    printf("size of rt3 = %d\n",sizeof(u.rt3));
    printf("size of union = %d\n",sizeof(u));

    subl(&u);
    if (u.rtl.rectype == 2)
            sub2(&u);
}
```

```
sub1(u)
union record *u;
{
}

sub2(u)
struct rectype2 *u;
{
    /* wrong declaration */
}


size of rt1 = 12    /* run on a 16-bit machine */
size of rt2 = 8
size of rt3 = 12
size of union = 12
```

Here, function sub2 incorrectly declares its argument to be a pointer to a record type 2 structure when a pointer to union type record was passed. On many implementations, both addresses may be exactly the same but using this idea with arrays of unions and/or structures will cause problems, as each element in an array of structures of rectype2 differs in size from an element of an arrays of union type record. Operations involving arithmetic on pointers to these elements (such as ++ and --) would return incorrect results, as the scaling factor used would be wrong. Interpreting arguments by other than their intended means is fraught with danger.

Like structures, unions may not contain instances of themselves but they can include pointers to instances of themselves. Unions may contain structures and structures can also contain unions.

Constructing Overlapping Arrays

For some applications it may be useful to have arrays that overlap, in whole or in part. In the following example, there are two integer arrays in which the last ten elements of one redefine the same data area as the first ten elements of the other.

```
/* union3.c - defining overlapping arrays. */

#include <stdio.h>

struct dummy {
    int filler[10];
    int iarray2[20];
};

union {
    struct dummy d;
    int iarray1[20];
} u;

main()
{
    printf("sizeof(u) = %d\n",sizeof(u));
}


sizeof(u) = 60 /* an int takes up 2 bytes */
```

This arrangement is inherently nonportable. Our earlier discussion about unions of structures with common leading members does not apply here and so storing something in iarray1[10] and retrieving it via iarray2[0] may not work for your particular implementation. If this idea works on your system then it is quite legitimate to use it, provided you understand its limitations.

Note the use of the variable filler. This definition is necessary to force the arrays to overlap properly. In FORTRAN, it is possible to have something like

```
      INTEGER*2    IARRY1(20)
      INTEGER*2    IARRY2(20)
      EQUIVALENCE  (IARRY1(1),IARRY2(11))
```

In this case, no filler is needed, as the language permits subarrays to be redefined. Because this is not possible in C, the `filler` array is necessary even though that field is never used. Such a field should be named carefully so there is little chance of it being used accidentally.

The idea of overlapping arrays can also be applied to character arrays, but it can cause some problems when dealing with strings.

```c
/* union4.c — overlapping string arrays. */

#include <stdio.h>
#include <string.h>

struct strings {
    char st1[2];
    char st2[4];
    char st3[6];
};

union {
    struct strings smlstr;
    char bigstr[12];
} u;

main()
{
    strcpy(u.bigstr,"hello there");
    printf("bigstr = >%s<\n",u.bigstr);
    printf("    st1 = >%s<\n",u.smlstr.st1);
    printf("    st2 = >%s<\n",u.smlstr.st2);
    printf("    st3 = >%s<\n",u.smlstr.st3);
}
```

```
bigstr = >hello there<
   st1 = >hello there<
   st2 = >llo there<
   st3 = >there<
```

Strings in C are stored as character arrays that have a terminating '\0'. This '\0' is required if the library string routines (including `printf`) are to work correctly. (This is a convention and need not be used unless it is necessary. That is, it is quite legitimate to have character strings without terminating '\0's, particularly if you store a length descriptor at the start or in some other variable.)

In the above example a 12 character string is redefined as three smaller strings. Note that we are dealing with strings here and not just character arrays and, therefore, we should take into account the terminating '\0' for each string. As the example shows, strings st1 and st2 are not terminated properly so displaying them using a printf mask of %s gives an unexpected result.

If a display mask of %.2s is used for st1 and %.4s is used with st2, the correct result is obtained but now st1 and st2 are being treated as nonterminated arrays, while st3 is '\0' terminated. This would work but the usage is not intuitively obvious. If you intend to deal with nonterminated strings, it is probably best to treat all strings that way rather than just some of them. (A better way to deal with substrings is to use the library routines strncpy and strncmp, which don't require strings to be '\0' terminated.)

Another technique of redefining arrays involves the use of pointers.

```
/* union5.c — alternate array overlap. */

#include <stdio.h>

int iarray[30];
int *iap1; /* ptr to start of array 1 */
int *iap2; /* ptr to start of array 2 */

main()
{
    iap1 = &iarray[0];
    iap2 = &iarray[10];

    iap1[15] = 12345;
    printf("iap2[5] = %d\n",iap2[5]);
}


iap2[5] = 12345
```

Here, one large array is used with two pointers that point to different parts within it, each of which corresponds to the start of a subarray. One interesting property of pointers and arrays is that pointers can be subscripted so that arrays can be implied any time a pointer is used. This method is portable whereas the earlier version, which used a union, is not, however, the union method is much more obvious to the programmer new to C. Once you become familiar with pointers, the pointer approach will become second nature.

This is another example of alternate ways to achieve some end with C. While having a choice of alternate approaches allows you to chose the methods you find easiest or most appropriate, it also means that you may have to maintain code written by others who use different techniques.

Union Initialization

Static and external structures can be initialized when they are defined, and it may seem reasonable to allow the same for unions. However, a union has only one of its members "active" at any one time, and it is up to the programmer to keep track of which member is the active one as this information is not inherently stored with the union itself. Therefore, at compile-time we do not have an active member since none has yet been used.

Given that it might be convenient to start off thinking that a union contains a particular member, it seems reasonable to allow an initialization as follows.

```
/* union6.c — illegal union initialization. */

union {
    long l;
    float f;
} u = {123.456};
```

By using an initial floating-point value the compiler should be able to understand that we are initializing the union u via member f. While some compilers do allow union initialization, this is nonportable. If it is allowed, it usually applies to the first declared member only, in which case if you wanted to initialize u.f as above the union declaration would need to be changed to

```
    union {
        float f;  /* must be declared first */
        long l;
    } u = {123.456};
```

Currently, the only portable way to initialize a union is to do so with run-time assignment statements.

Each member of a `static` and external structure is initialized to zero by default and the same is true for members of unions.

```
/* union7.c - displaying union initial values. */

#include <stdio.h>

union u {
    long l;
    float f;
};

union u u1;

main()
{
    static union u u2;

    printf("u1.l = %ld\n",u1.l);
    printf("u1.f = %3.1f\n",u1.f);
    printf("u2.l = %ld\n",u1.l);
    printf("u2.f = %3.1f\n",u1.f);
}


u1.l = 0
u1.f = 0.0
u2.l = 0
u2.f = 0.0
```

The results of this example may be misleading. On the machine used, a float variable is stored in 4 bytes and a value of zero is actually represented by 4 bytes, each containing binary zero. The binary representation of float (or double) zero may vary from one machine to another, in which case initializing a union with binary bytes may result in nonzero values for certain object types. So it may be erroneous to assume that such values will initially have a numerical value of zero. (calloc initializes allocated space as "all bits zero".)

Unions and Alignment

Unions have the same alignment requirements as structures. A union starts and ends on the same type of boundary so that arrays of unions can be implemented, and that boundary is at least as strict as the one required by the members in the union. (It may be more strict.) Aggregate alignment is discussed earlier in this chapter in the section on Structures.

It may be advantageous on certain machines to force stricter alignment than would otherwise result as the default. The following example shows how this may be achieved.

```
/* union8.c — forcing variable alignment. */

union {
    long l;
    char ca[1000];
} u1;

struct st {
    short si;
    char c[6];
};

union {
    double d;
    struct st s[20];
} u2;
```

If it is desirable to have a 1000-element character array begin on a long int boundary, that array can be equivalenced with a long int via a union.

The variable l is never used in the program, it only serves to force the array's starting alignment.

In the second union, there exists an array of twenty structures, each element of which is 8 bytes long (on a machine with 2-byte short ints). If the size of a double is also 8 bytes, then we may be able to speed up accesses to that array in certain environments and for operations such as structure assignment.

Internal Storage Layouts

For some applications it is useful to know exactly how bytes and words are packed into longwords or quadwords. The following example gives the byte and word (16 bits) order in a longword (32 bits).

```
/* union9.c - inspecting byte and word ordering. */

#include <stdio.h>

#define SIZE (sizeof(long)/sizeof(char))

union {
    long longint;
    char ca[SIZE];
} u;

main()
{
    int i;

    u.longint = 0x01234567;

    for (i = 0; i < SIZE; i++)
            printf("ca[%d] = %02x\n",
                    i,u.ca[i]);
}


ca[0] = 67 /* one possible result */
```

```
ca[1] = 45
ca[2] = 23
ca[3] = 01
```

The same mechanism can be used to display internal floating point representations in hexadecimal (or some other form).

```
/* union10.c - float/long redefinition */

#include <stdio.h>

union {
    float f;
    long l;
} u;

main()
{
    for (u.f = -5.0; u.f <= 5.0; ++u.f)
      printf("u.f = %5.1f (FP), %08lx (hex)\n",
             u.f,u.l);
}
```

```
u.f = -5.0 (FP), C0A00000 (hex)
u.f = -4.0 (FP), C0800000 (hex)
u.f = -3.0 (FP), C0400000 (hex)
u.f = -2.0 (FP), C0000000 (hex)
u.f = -1.0 (FP), BF800000 (hex)
u.f =  0.0 (FP), 00000000 (hex)
u.f =  1.0 (FP), 3F800000 (hex)
u.f =  2.0 (FP), 40000000 (hex)
u.f =  3.0 (FP), 40400000 (hex)
u.f =  4.0 (FP), 40800000 (hex)
u.f =  5.0 (FP), 40A00000 (hex)
```

On many 16-bit machines, a long int and a float both take up 4 bytes as shown above. You may need to modify this program for your system.

A Binary Display Program

Occasionally it is useful to be able to display values using a binary radix, and because printf does not support such a mask, you will need to write your own facility. The following program is not terribly elegant but it does the job and reinforces the concept of fields and unions.

```
/* union11.c - 16-bit word to binary display */

#include <stdio.h>

struct mask {
    unsigned hi_bit : 1;
    unsigned        : 15;
};

union {
    struct mask word;
    int i;
} u;

main()
{
    int i, j;

    for (i = -5; i <= 5; ++i) {
            printf("i = %3d (dec), ",i);
            u.i = i;
            j = 16;
            while (j--) {
                    printf("%d",u.word.hi_bit);
                    u.i <<= 1;
            }
            puts(" (bin)");
    }
}
```

```
i = -5 (dec), 1111111111111011 (bin)
i = -4 (dec), 1111111111111100 (bin)
i = -3 (dec), 1111111111111101 (bin)
i = -2 (dec), 1111111111111110 (bin)
i = -1 (dec), 1111111111111111 (bin)
```

```
i = 0 (dec), 0000000000000000 (bin)
i = 1 (dec), 0000000000000001 (bin)
i = 2 (dec), 0000000000000010 (bin)
i = 3 (dec), 0000000000000011 (bin)
i = 4 (dec), 0000000000000100 (bin)
i = 5 (dec), 0000000000000101 (bin)
```

The compiler used for this example stored the first bit field in the high bit. If your compiler stores it in the low bit, you will need to swap the order of the two bit fields. Obviously, this code is not portable.

The X3J11 Draft

The proposed draft Standard contains the following comments about unions.

- Each union has a separate name-space so the same member name can exist in multiple unions definitions without conflict. K&R allowed this provided certain offset considerations were obeyed. The K&R approach was enforced in UNIX Version 7–era compilers and is still implemented by a number of popular compilers.

- Unions can be assigned using u1 = u2 provided that both the unions u1 and u2 are of the same type.

```
/* union12.c - union assignment. */

union u1 {
    long longint;
    char c;
};

union u2 {
    long li;
    char ch;
};

main()
{
    union u1 union1, union2;
    union u2 union3;

    union1 = union2;
    union3 = union1;          /* ??? */
    union3 = (u2) union1;
}
```

Because union1 and union2 are of the same type, they can be copied to each other. While the layout of union3 and union1 is identical, strictly speaking, they are not the same type, so the second assignment above may generate an error. By casting union1 to type u2, the assignment should work, although it might not be strictly portable (at least in theory).

- Unions may be passed to functions as arguments and returned as function return values. This will break existing code if it doesn't use &union-name when passing a union pointer. In future, the & operator will be necessary when passing union pointers.

```
/* union13.c - unions and functions. */

union {
    long l;
    char c;
} u1, u2, *pu;
```

```
main()
{
    /* ... */
    u2 = f(ul);        /* pass and return by value */
    pu = g(&ul);       /* pass and return by address */
}
```

- External and static unions may be initialized at definition time and the initializing list is interpreted according to the first member in the definition.

CHAPTER 2

Arrays

Arrays are a very natural and common way of dealing with multiple occurrences of a variable. Arrays are so common that they are often taken for granted. Once programmers have learned how to construct and use them for one programming language, they often assume arrays behave the same way in other languages, but this clearly is not the case. Some languages store multidimensional arrays by row, others by column. Some pass array arguments by address, others by value. Some support the notion of arrays of pointers, while others do not.

C provides the usual array constructs that one might expect from common high-level languages. Given this, most algorithms can be implemented in C in much the same way as for many other languages. However, arrays in C have some interesting properties and restrictions that may require a different approach to coding than is commonplace in other languages.

Array Initialization

Most languages allow variables (including arrays) to be initialized at compile-time and/or run-time and C is no exception. The appropriate time for this initialization depends on a number of factors. Generally, initialization at compile-time will lengthen the compilation time but does not penalize the program at run-time. Run-time initialization can have the opposite effect of making the compilation quicker, slowing execution time and increasing the program size.

If any algorithm is used to initialize variables, initialization must be performed at run-time so that the results can be computed. (Note that `auto` variables in C, which may contain any executable initializing expression, are initialized at run-time, not compile-time.)

47

The following example initializes a 4x4 integer array such that every element has the value 1. Both C and FORTRAN versions are shown.

Compile-Time Initialization

```
/* array1.c - compile-time initialization */

int iarray[4][4] =
    {1,1,1,1},
    {1,1,1,1},
    {1,1,1,1},
    {1,1,1,1}
};

/*
    INTEGER*2 IARRAY(4,4)

    DATA IARRAY /4*1,4*1,4*1,4*1/
*/
```

C stores consecutive elements of arrays in contiguous memory locations and multidimensional arrays are stored in row-major order. Therefore, in the above example, the elements of iarray are stored as [0][0], ..., [0][3], [1][0], ..., [1][3], ..., [3][3]. The list of initial values has been broken into four sets of four values and has been written such that it exactly matches the way in which one would logically imagine the array to exist. The list could also have been written

```
int iarray[4][4] = {
    {1,1,1,1},{1,1,1,1},{1,1,1,1},{1,1,1,1}
};
```

and while this has exactly the same meaning, it is more difficult to visualize. The braces around each of the four sets of values are optional and the initializer list may be written as follows.

```
int iarray[4][4] = {
    1,1,1,1,1,1,1,1,1,1,1,1,1,1,1,1
};
```

This example has no implied array structure information whatsoever and is the worst way of writing such a definition.

If `iarray` were equated with a 16-element single-dimensional array called `earray`, the four rows of `iarray` would appear to be concatenated into one big list and could be accessed as `earray[0]` ..., `earray[15]`.

Redefining a multidimensional array as a single dimensional array is usually done for convenience. By reducing different multidimensional arrays to one-dimensional lists, their elements can all be processed by the same function. Such redefinition can also make array initialization easier (although not necessarily clearer). For example, FORTRAN allows consecutive elements in an array to be initialized with the same value, as follows.

```
DATA IARRAY /16*1/
```

This abbreviated method is not supported by C.

There is a potential conflict between array redefinition in C and compile-time initialization which results from using a union with an initialization list.

```
/* array2.c - definition/initialization conflict */

union u {
    int iarray[4][4];
    int earray[16];
} = {
    { 1, 2, 3, 4},
    { 5, 6, 7, 8},
    { 9,10,11,12},
    {13,14,15,16}
};
```

Many compilers do not permit an initialization list to be used in conjunction with a union. Those compilers that do, usually interpret the list according to the definition of the first member of the union. The problem can be solved at compile-time using a pointer instead of a single-dimensional array. This approach works well, is not complicated, and is not dependent on your compiler supporting union initialization.

```
/* array3.c - redefinition using pointers */

#include <stdio.h>

int iarray[4][4] = {
    { 1, 2, 3, 4},
    { 5, 6, 7, 8},
    { 9,10,11,12},
    {13,14,15,16}
};

int *earray = &iarray[0][0];

main()
{
    int i;

    for (i = 0; i <= 15; ++i)
            printf("earray[%2d] = %d\n",
                    i,earray[i]);
}
```

```
earray[ 0] = 1
earray[ 1] = 2
        . . .
earray[14] = 15
earray[15] = 16
```

Run-Time Initialization

Initializing at run-time allows much more complicated initialization expressions than does compile-time initialization.

```
/* array4.c - run-time initialization */

int iarray[4][4];

main()
{
    int i,j;

    for (i = 0; i < 4; i++)
            for (j = 0; j < 4; j++)
                    iarray[i][j] = 1;
}
```

Using the knowledge of internal array storage discussed earlier, a short cut can be taken which results in only one loop and uses a pointer instead of subscripts.

```
/* array5.c - run-time init alternate */

#define ROW 4
#define COL 4

int ia[ROW][COL];

main()
{
    int *pi;

    for (pi = &ia[0][0];
         pi <= &ia[ROW - 1][COL - 1]; ++pi)
            *pi = 1;
}
```

Initializing Sparse Matrices

Consider the case of initializing an identity matrix at compile-time. (Throughout this chapter the mathematical concept of matrices will be used in examples. Since an array can be used to represent a matrix, the terms *array* and *matrix* will be used interchangeably.)

```
/* array6.c - initializing sparse matrices */
int sarray[6][6] = {
    {1,0,0,0,0,0},
    {0,1,0,0,0,0},
    {0,0,1,0,0,0},
    {0,0,0,1,0,0},
    {0,0,0,0,1,0},
    {0,0,0,0,0,1}
};

int tarray[6][6] = {
    {1},
    {0,1},
    {0,0,1},
```

```
      {0,0,0,1},
      {0,0,0,0,1}
      {0,0,0,0,0,1},
   };
```

These examples are equivalent. They both result in a 6x6 identity matrix. The two approaches look quite similar except that the first one explicitly gives all element values while the second lets trailing column values default to zero. While the choice between them is largely subjective, the former is very obviously an identity matrix whereas the latter requires some knowledge of default values.

Default Initialization

If an external or internal `static` object is not explicitly initialized (using a constant expression), it is implicitly initialized as if every scalar member in the object were assigned the integer constant zero.

```c
/* array7.c — default initialization */

char ec[10];
int ei[100];
struct s {
    int i;
    char c[6];
} estr[5];

main()
{
    static char sc[5];
    static long sl[10];
    static struct s sstr[4];

    auto int ai[20];
    auto struct s astr[3];
}
```

In the above example, every element of the external or `static` arrays is set to zero. Therefore, such arrays not explicitly initialized become zero matrices. (The contents of elements of the `auto` arrays are unpredictable.)

Often, `char` arrays contain text strings, which by convention are terminated by a `'\0'`. Therefore, it might seem sufficient for a compiler to set the first element only in such an array to `'\0'`, leaving the remainder undefined. However, `char` arrays need not be accessed as strings; the programmer is quite at liberty to store any bit pattern in a `char` that will fit and to access the elements in any order. Because the compiler can't always decide as to how a `char` array will be used, it must set all elements of `char` arrays to zero.

`char` Array Initialization

There are a number of ways to specify the list of initializers for a `char` array that is to contain a string.

```
/* array8.c — char array initialization */

char c1[] = {'h','e','l','l','o','\0'};
char c2[6] = {'h','e','l','l','o'};
char c3[] = {"hello"};
char c4[] = "hello";
char c5[5] = "hello";
```

In the first example, the list of initializing characters is enclosed in braces and the compiler dimensions the array c1 according to the number of values in the list. Array c2 is explicitly dimensioned to six and the list contains five values with the sixth defaulting to zero ('\0'). This method is very error prone. Arrays c3 and c4 are identical as the enclosing braces in c3 are optional. As for c1, the compiler calculates the length of the array needed to store the list.

The final example deserves a special mention. Like c2, it specifies both a size and a list of initializers but whereas c2's list was shorter than the array size, the list for c5 has exactly the same number of values as the declared size. Just what is stored in c5? If a literal string is used to initialize a char array, successive characters in the literal are stored in the array. If the array has no explicit size, the whole literal, including trailing '\0' is copied. If an explicit size is given, as is the case for c5, only that many characters are copied. If there is no room for the trailing '\0', it is *not* copied. Therefore, c5 is not terminated properly and cannot predictably be used as a string.

Initializing Arrays of Pointers

Many C experts argue that because of C's ability to handle arrays of pointers, there is little or no need to use multidimensional arrays. Depending on the speed and efficiency requirements and the ease-of-maintenance concerns, both approaches to nonlinear data storage may be reasonable. There is no cut and dried rule for their selection except that, perhaps, arrays of literal strings are more efficiently handled using arrays of char pointers than multidimensional char arrays, as the latter approach requires all strings to be the same length whereas the former does not.

```
/* array9.c - initializing arrays of pointers */

#include <stdio.h>

main()
{
    static char *part1[] = {
            "screw",
            "big blue bolt",
            "widget",
            "red wheel"
    };

#if 0       /* exclude the following code */
/* error in {'s'...'w'} */

    static char *part2[] = {
            {'s','c','r','e','w'},
            "big blue bolt",
            "widget",
            "red wheel"
    };

/* error in {1...5} */

    static int *value1[] =
            {5,1,2,3,4,5},
            {3,100,200,300},
            {1,-4},
            {4,-1,4,7,9},
            {0}
    };
#endif
    static int i1[] = {5,1,2,3,4,5};
    static int i2[] = {3,100,200,300};
    static int i3[] = {1,-4};
    static int i4[] = {4,-1,4,7,9};
    static int i5[] = {0};

    static int *value2[] = {i1,i2,i3,i4,i5};

    printf("*value2[0] = %d\n",*value2[0]);
    printf("*(value2[1] + 3) = %d\n",*(value2[1] + 3));
    printf("(value2[1])[3] = %d\n",(value2[1])[3]);
```

```
    printf("(value2[3])[3] = %d\n",(value2[3])[3]);
}
```

```
*value2[0] = 5
*(value2[1] + 3) = 300
(value2[1])[3] = 300
(value2[3])[3] = 7
```

Array part1 is a list of pointers to char strings. The compiler allocates space for the strings and stores each starting address in the corresponding element of part1. This same technique can be used at run-time by allocating storage via malloc or calloc and storing the pointer in an array. (In this case, be sure to cast the returned pointer to the required type before storing it in the array.)

The example also attempts to initialize array part2 to be equivalent to part1. Literal strings can be used as shorthand initializer lists for single-dimensional arrays. In such a case, "screw" is identical to {'s','c','r','e','w'}. However, this is not true for arrays of pointers because {'s',... 'w'} is not an expression equivalent to a char pointer whereas "screw" is. In this example, each value 's',... 'w' is considered to correspond to a different element of part2.

What was really attempted with part2 was to define a list of initial values, hoping that they would be magically stored somewhere and that the address of that list would be stored in the pointer array. This didn't happen with part2 and it doesn't work with the lists of integers in value1 either. Clearly some other approach is needed.

Array value2 contains a list of pointers to arrays of integers. Because these lists cannot be defined at the same time value2 is initialized, these integer arrays are defined first and pointers to them are assigned to elements of value2.

With an array of pointers to arrays of integers, how are these integers referenced? Element value2[0] contains the address of the first integer array and this is synonymous with the address of the first integer within that array. Therefore, *value2[0] refers to the contents of the first element in the first integer array.

To get at the fourth element in the second array *(value2[1] + 3) is used. The fourth element is at offset 3 from the start of the second array.

The same element can be referenced using (value2[1])[3]). The term (value2[1]) is a pointer, and as has already been demonstrated, pointers can be subscripted. Actually, the parentheses can be omitted leaving value2[1][3], which looks exactly like a two-dimensional array reference (which in a logical sense it is because a two-dimensional is a one-dimensional array, each of whose elements is another one-dimensional array). Likewise, the expression (value2[3])[3]) refers to the fourth element in the fourth array.

It is worth commenting on the methods used to terminate arrays of pointers (and arrays in general). In value2 above, the first element in each integer array contains the number of integers following it in that array. Using this count, the end of each integer array can be determined. A special array of zero values has been used to indicate the end of value2.

Likewise, each string in part1 is terminated by the trailing '\0', but the array part1 is not terminated in any predictable way. A final initializer of "" could be appended so that the end of part1 is reached when a pointer to a null string is reached.

The use of a pointer to a zero array or null string may be practical for some applications but will prove insufficient if zero value arrays and/or null strings are valid occurrences. This is particularly likely in applications where the arrays pointed to are constructed at run-time. In this case, it would be better to terminate the pointer array with the NULL pointer as in

```
static int *value2[] = {i1,i2,i3,i4,NULL};
```

Negative Subscripting

One so-called weakness in C, particularly when it is compared with Pascal, is that arrays must always begin with subscript zero. On closer inspection, that need not be true. Actually, it can be quite legitimate (and portable) to use negative subscripts although there are some limitations.

```
/* array10.c - negative subscripting */

#include <stdio.h>

int i[] = {0,1,2,3,4,5,6,7,8,9,10};

main()
{
    int *pi = &i[5];
    int j;

    for (j = -5; j <= 5; ++j)
            printf("x[%2d] = %2d\n",j,pi[j]);
}


x[-5] = 0
x[-4] = 1
x[-3] = 2
x[-2] = 3
x[-1] = 4
x[ 0] = 5
x[ 1] = 6
x[ 2] = 7
x[ 3] = 8
x[ 4] = 9
x[ 5] = 10
```

The array i contains the eleven elements i[0], ..., i[10], and it is desired to use the elements as though they were defined as i[-5], ..., i[5] because that is a better fit for a particular application.

Array references such as i[j] actually translate to *(i + j). The value of j is scaled to the object type that i points to and the new value is added to i giving the address required. Numerous examples have shown the subscripting of pointers so by making pi point to the middle element of array i, pi now becomes the origin of a new array; one that is accessed via pi rather than i. The elements of the "array" pi can be accessed using pi[k] provided that −5<=k<=5. Outside of these bounds, array i no longer exists and, hence, any mapping of it into pi is no longer meaningful. Similarly, by using int *pi = &i[2];, pi[k] is valid for −2<=k<=8.

The key thing to remember is that while k remains within the bounds of i, the technique is safe and portable. If i is to be accessed as pi[1], pi[2], ..., pi[11] something like int *pi = &i[-1]; is required. Likewise, pi[100], ..., pi[110] would require int *pi = &i[-100];. Both of these examples will work on a large number of implementations, but this technique is not guaranteed and therefore is not portable. Because i is being referenced outside of its bounds, C makes no guarantee that such a reference is meaningful. One obvious problem is that if i is the first object stored in a memory segment or in the heap then referencing an address before its beginning may result in strange results when unsigned pointer arithmetic is used to locate a subsequent offset. It may even result in a fatal run-time error due to a "memory violation."

A similar problem will occur if pi is to be accessed with only negative subscripts such as pi[-20], pi[-19], ..., pi[-10].

Consider the case of an x–y coordinate system that is to be viewed as a two dimensional array using negative and positive subscripts for either or both of x and y (row and column). Will the technique shown above work for two dimensions?

```
/* array11.c - negative subscripting in 2D */

#include <stdio.h>

int i[5][5] = {
    { 1,  2,  3,  4,  5},
    { 6,  7,  8,  9,  0},
    {-1,-2,-3,-4,-5},
    {-6,-7,-8,-9, 0},
    { 1,  2,  3,  4,  5}
};

main()
{
    int *px = &i[2][2];
    int *py = &i[1][0];
    int j,k;

    for (j = -2; j <= 2; ++j)
        for (k = -2; k <= 2; ++k)
            printf("x[%2d][%2d] = %2d\n",
                    j,k,px[j][k]);
```

```
/* compilation error on px[j][k] reference */

    for (j = -1; j <= 3; ++j)
        for (k = 0; k <= 4; ++k)
            printf("y[%2d][%2d] = %2d\n",
                        j,k,py[j][k]);

/* compilation error on py[j][k] reference */
}
```

The object of this example is to redefine the array i (which has $0<=x<=4$) such that px[x][y] has $-2<=x<=2$, $-2<=y<=2$ and py[x][y] has $-1<=x<=3$, $1<=y<=4$. The expressions px[j][k] and py[j][k] generate compilation errors because px and py were never declared as arrays. Although it is legal to subscript a pointer such as px or py, this only applies to using a one-dimensional subscript. The expression px[4] results in an address four objects beyond the beginning of px. However, the expression px[4][5] is meaningless. Unless px was declared as an array, the compiler has no idea of the array's row size and so it cannot generate the proper offset for this reference.

Because the problem lies in the method used to reference these pseudoarrays, it seems reasonable to experiment with a different approach.

```
/* array12.c - more negative subscripting */

#include <stdio.h>

int i[5][5] = {
   { 1, 2, 3, 4, 5},
   { 6, 7, 8, 9, 0},
   {-1,-2,-3,-4,-5},
   {-6,-7,-8,-9, 0},
   { 1, 2, 3, 4, 5}
};

main()
{
   int *px = &i[2][2];
   int j,k;

   for (j = -2; j <= 2; ++j)
       for (k = -2; k <= 2; ++k) {
           printf("x[%2d][%2d] = %2d, %2d\n",
               j,k,(px+(j*5))[k],*(px+(j*5)+k));
           }
}
```

```
x[-2][-2] =  1,  1
x[-2][-1] =  2,  2
x[-2][ 0] =  3,  3
x[-2][ 1] =  4,  4
x[-2][ 2] =  5,  5
x[-1][-2] =  6,  6
x[-1][-1] =  7,  7
x[-1][ 0] =  8,  8
x[-1][ 1] =  9,  9
x[-1][ 2] =  0,  0
x[ 0][-2] = -1, -1
x[ 0][-1] = -2, -2
x[ 0][ 0] = -3, -3
x[ 0][ 1] = -4, -4
x[ 0][ 2] = -5, -5
x[ 1][-2] = -6, -6
x[ 1][-1] = -7, -7
x[ 1][ 0] = -8, -8
x[ 1][ 1] = -9, -9
```

```
x[ 1][ 2] =  0,  0
x[ 2][-2] =  1,  1
x[ 2][-1] =  2,  2
x[ 2][ 0] =  3,  3
x[ 2][ 1] =  4,  4
x[ 2][ 2] =  5,  5
```

Success. By taking the actual size of the array i into account, the desired results can be obtained. This example only shows the case for px. Using other mappings of i, such as in py discussed earlier, requires a simple change to this program.

The expressions *(px+(j*5)+k) and (px+(j*5))[k] are identical; both return the contents of px[j][k]. In the former, (px+(j*5)+k) involves the scaling of the row subscript so that an element offset can be found. This is in turn scaled by the type of the pointer resulting in the absolute address of the requested element. In the latter case, (px+(j*5)) results in a pointer, and as pointers can be subscripted, (px+(j*5))[k] references the contents of the desired location. Again, this reinforces the fact that two-dimensional arrays are one dimensional arrays, each of whose elements is another one dimensional array.

The expressions for specifying elements in the pseudoarray px are messy and their meaning is not obvious. This can be simplified by the use of a macro of the form PX(a,b) which expands to an expression to reference the element at row a, column b.

Arrays as Function Arguments

In C, arrays are always passed to functions by address. It is not possible to pass an array by value. Under certain circumstances, it is permissible to omit the most significant dimension from an array declaration.

```
/* array13.c - omitting the first dimension */

#include <stdio.h>

int k[] = {1,2,3,4,5};
long l[][3] = {
    {1,2,3},
    {4,5,6}
};

main()
{
    double d[10];
    int i[2][3][4];

    printf("sizeof k = %d\n",sizeof(k));
    printf("sizeof l = %d\n",sizeof(l));
    printf("sizeof d = %d\n",sizeof(d));
    printf("sizeof i = %d\n\n",sizeof(i));
    sub(d,i,i);
}

sub(d,i,j)
double d[];
int i[2][3][4];
int j[][3][4];
{
    printf("sizeof d = %d\n",sizeof(d));
    printf("sizeof i = %d\n",sizeof(i));
    printf("sizeof j = %d\n",sizeof(j));
}


sizeof k = 10
sizeof l = 24
sizeof d = 80
sizeof i = 48

sizeof d = 2
sizeof i = 2
sizeof j = 2
```

The array k has no explicit size and as the compiler finds five values in the initialization list, it uses 5 as the array dimension. Similarly, the major subscript was omitted from array l and the compiler sets this to 2. In this case the compiler can deduce the number of rows in l from the initializing value list but it still needs the number of columns. If the braces in the list were omitted, it could still deduce the number of rows. (Note that in that case, all initial values must be listed; they cannot default to zero as is possible when using the { . . . }, { . . . }, . . . format.)

The results of the first four sizeofs are as expected, but the next three might not be expected, although they are correct (at least for an implementation that uses 2-byte pointers). The function call sub(d,i,i); passes three arguments to function sub, namely, &d[0], &i[0][0][0], and &i[0][0][0]. No information regarding the sizes of these arrays is passed.

In function sub, d is declared as a pointer to a double while i and j are declared to point to integers. They are *not* array declarations. The [. . .] expressions are only present to indicate the dimensions of any array that might begin at that address; they do not indicate how much storage (if any) is allocated at that address. Because d, i, and j are declared as pointers to objects of type double, int, and int respectively, then using them with the sizeof operator results in the size of those pointers, not the arrays that they might point to.

The declaration for j is quite valid. The first dimension can be omitted as it is not needed when scaling and producing element offsets. Because arrays are passed by address it would seem reasonable to assume that subparts of an array could be passed using the address of the beginning of that subpart.

```
/* array14.c - passing subarrays */

#include <stdio.h>

main()
{
   static char c[] = "hello there";
   static char d[3][5] = {
           {"frog"},
           {"tree"},
           {"blue"}
   };
   static char e[2][2][3] = {
           {"ab","cd"},
           {"lm","no"}
   };

   sub(c[5],&c[5]);
   sub(d[1][0],&d[1][0]);
   sub(e[0][1][0],&e[0][1][0]);
}

sub(c,ca)
char c;
char ca[];
{
   printf("  char = '%c'\n",c);
   printf("string = \"%s\"\n\n",ca);
}


  char = ' '
string = " there"

  char = 't'
string = "tree"

  char = 'c'
string = "cd"
```

Function sub expects a character and a character pointer as its arguments. Array c is a char array containing a null terminated string, so &c[5] points to the beginning of a trailing substring within c. This substring is terminated by the same '\0' that terminates c. By passing a&c[5] we have effectively passed the address of a trailing subarray within the array c.

Arrays d and e look like arrays of pointer to char strings but they are two- and three-dimensional arrays of characters that just happen to use the shorthand notation for an initializer list. Note that space has been reserved in the dimensions for the '\0' terminator.

Passing trailing substrings is easy because the terminating '\0' is present to indicate where the array ends. However, this is not so if it is desired to pass a leading or midpart substring or part of a non-char array. In all of these cases, a value must be passed that indicates the length of the subarray. Due to the way in which multidimensional arrays are stored, the technique fails with this type of array.

```
/* array15.c - 2 dimensional array subsets */

#include <stdio.h>

main()
{
    static int i[5][4] = {
            { 1, 2, 3, 4},
            { 5, 6, 7, 8},
            { 9,10,11,12},
            {13,14,15,16},
            {17,18,19,20}
    };

    sub(&i[0][0]);
    sub(&i[2][0]);
    sub(&i[3][2]);
}

sub(i)
int i[2][2];
{
    printf("\n      [0]    [1]\n");
    printf("[0]  %2d    %2d\n",i[0][0],i[0][1]);
    printf("[1]  %2d    %2d\n",i[1][0],i[1][1]);
}
```

(actual output)   (desired output)

```
     [0]  [1]              [0]  [1]
[0]   1    2          [0]   1    2
[1]   3    4          [1]   5    6

     [0]  [1]              [0]  [1]
[0]   9   10          [0]   9   10
[1]  11   12          [1]  13   14

     [0]  [1]              [0]  [1]
[0]  15   16          [0]  15   16
[1]  17   18          [1]  19   20
```

The intent here is to have a function `sub` that can handle any 2x2 array passed to it. By passing different addresses within the array `i` in main, `i` could be dealt with as a series of 2x2 subarrays. Unfortunately, as the output shows, this isn't the case even though the address passed is the address of the required subarray. The declaration of `i` in `main` and `i` in `sub` have no relationship and all offsets within `i` in `sub` are really offsets in `i` in `main` and depend on the order of element storage in `main` not `sub`.

Miscellaneous Notes

C places no limit on the number of dimensions allowed with arrays (although specific implementations of C may). Even when an array is defined or declared with a given number of dimensions, references to that array may include less than the maximum number of subscripts. When a five dimensional array `fda` is passed by address to a function, the argument used is usually `sub(fda);`, although `sub(&fda[0][0][0][0][0]);` could be used instead. This is obviously a case of referencing `fda` with less than five subscripts, but the array is being referenced as a whole so no subscripts are required. Could something like `fda[1][3][4]` be used?

```
/* array16.c — addressing rows and columns */

#include <stdio.h>

main()
{
    static int i[2][3][2] = {
            {{ 1,  2},{ 3,  4},{ 5,  6}},
            {{ 7,  8},{ 9,10},{11,12}}
    };

    printf("            i = %u\n",i);
    printf("&i[0][0][0] = %u\n",&i[0][0][0]);
    printf("       *i[1] = %u\n",*i[1]);
    printf("    i[1][0] = %u\n",i[1][0]);
    printf("      **i[1] = %2d\n",**i[1]);
    printf("   *i[1][0] = %2d\n",*i[1][0]);
    printf(" i[1][0][0] = %2d\n",i[1][0][0]);
}



            i = 210
  &i[0][0][0] = 210
       *i[1] = 222
     i[1][0] = 222
      **i[1] = 7
    *i[1][0] = 7
  i[1][0][0] = 7
```

In this example, i is a three dimensional array and the whole array or parts of it can be legitimately referenced using 0, 1, 2, or 3 subscripts (which is something that many common languages don't allow). As shown, i and &i[0][0][0] both refer to the address of the first element in i. (210 just happens to be the address of this object on the implementation used.) The element i[1] is another array which itself contains elements each of which is an array. So i[1] is the address of an array as is i[0]. The array pointed to by i[0] is immediately followed in memory by the array pointed to by i[1]. If ints are stored as 2 bytes, then each of these subarrays is 3x2 ints or 12 bytes long and i[1] equals i[0] + 12 bytes (i.e., 222 equals 210 + 12).

Because i[0] points to an array and a pointer to an array is equivalent to a pointer to the first object in that array, the expressions *i[1] and i[1][0] are equivalent. Likewise, the expressions **i[1], *i[1][0], and i[1][0][0] are equivalent. As demonstrated, array references can contain less than the maximum number of subscripts.

Pointers can be subscripted, and as a string literal is a pointer expression, it might be expected that a literal could be subscripted as follows:

```
/* array17.c - more on subscripting pointers */

#include <stdio.h>

main()
{
    int i;

    for (i = 0; i < 6; i++)
            printf("x[%d] = '%c'\n",i,"abcdef"[i]);
}


x[0] = 'a'
x[1] = 'b'
x[2] = 'c'
x[3] = 'd'
x[4] = 'e'
x[5] = 'f'
```

The technique works; however, it is difficult to think of a reasonable application for it. If the literal expression is used in multiple places throughout a program, each instance of it would be treated as a completely new literal and would require extra storage, whereas if it were an external char array (or passed as a function argument by pointer), this overhead would be eliminated.

The only operator that can be applied to an array is sizeof. C has no support for matrix operations as do some versions of BASIC.

What is the maximum number of elements in an array? Is this value an int or long and is it signed? The answers to these are implementation specific, so the safest thing is to find out what your implementation does or to design a generic and portable algorithm. (You may need to be concerned with these answers if you have an array that is to contain object lengths as returned by sizeof.)

Some languages support the idea of variable length arrays. The best way to imitate these is by using the malloc and calloc library functions, which allow arrays of a given size to be created on the heap dynamically at run-time.

Machines such as the DEC PDP-11 support object module overlaying in order to have programs larger than 64KB. Under DEC's RSX family of operating systems, each time a disk overlay is loaded (or reloaded), all of its data areas are reinitialized to their compile-time values (unless they are defined in some root area such as provided for in FORTRAN's COMMON). If you are working on a machine with similar behavior, you may need to reevaluate your decision regarding compile-time versus run-time initialization, particularly if your application works without overlays, yet when you overlay it, it fails.

The X3J11 Draft

A number of points regarding the proposed ANSI Standard are worth mentioning. They are:

- Unions can be initialized provided that the initializer list pertains to the first member defined in the union.

- typedef size_t is defined in the standard header file stddef.h. size_t is described as the integral type of the result of the sizeof operator. Even if you are using a nonconforming compiler you can use this pseudotype to write portable code by defining size_t to correspond to the type of your implementation's sizeof return value.

- The macro NULL may be defined in the standard header stddef.h as 0, 0L, or

```
#define NULL (void *)0
```

- The latter is read as "the value zero cast into a pointer to type void." A pointer to type void is a pointer of such alignment and length that it can be cast to and from any other pointer type without losing any information. In most implementations it will be like a pointer to char. One particular use for pointer to void is that this will be the type of the pointers returned from the library functions malloc, calloc, and realloc.

- The notion of pointer to void is related to the idea that pointers to different types of objects need not be the same size and in future implementations, pointer conversion and alignment rules may cause existing code to break. Pointers to void have no relation whatsoever to functions of type void. The later indicates that the function does not return a value and this has nothing to do with pointers.

- Arrays cannot be passed to or returned by functions.

- The constant expression that specifies the size of an array must be of integral type and positive value.

CHAPTER 3

Function Definition, Reference, and Pointers

One of the fundamental concepts of the C language is that of the function. Most compiled languages support the notion of separate modules of executable code that can be called by each other (and in the case of recursion, by themselves). While this mechanism is common and well known to most professional programmers, its implementation in C is worth commenting on for several reasons.

First, languages such as BASIC and FORTRAN allow both subroutines and functions. In these languages subroutines may take and return arguments, and functions may take arguments but can only return one value and then only through the function name itself (i.e., A = ABS(x), B = SIN(y)). In C, a function may optionally pass and/or return values via arguments and it may also optionally return a value via the function's name. It may behave like a traditional subroutine or a function or both.

Second, most languages differentiate between a main program and its subordinate routines. In C, all modules are called functions and they all have the same structure. While the main function of a C program must be called main, this is an arbitrary choice and any function name could have been used. (Refer to the discussion of program startup in Chapter 6 for further details.) Function main looks like any other C function and can be called by itself or any other function. While main is rarely called from within a user program, it is always called by the vendor-supplied program startup module.

While it is possible to write large amounts of useful code without an intimate understanding of C's function definition and calling mechanism, some knowledge will prove useful. (For a discussion on argument passing via a stack frame, see Chapter 4.)

Actual and Formal Arguments

Arguments present in the list used when a function is called are actual arguments, whereas those present in a function definition are formal (or dummy) arguments.

In most function definition examples, the arguments are usually declared in the same order that they appear in the formal list. This ordering is unnecessary as arguments may be declared in any order and some need not be declared at all.

```
/* functl.c - formal argument declaration order */

sub(a,b,c,d)
int b;
double d;
long a;
{
    /* ... */
}
```

The order of formal arguments in the function definition is a, b, c, and d but the order of their declaration is b, d, and a. Argument c is not declared at all so it defaults to type int. (Default typing can be difficult to spot and is not recommended.)

When an array is used as an actual argument, the argument becomes the address of the first element in that array (except when an array is used with sizeof, but then sizeof is not a function, it is a compile-time operator.) In this case, an array's name is synonymous with a pointer to that array.

```
/* funct2.c - pointer and array arguments */

main()
{
    char c[20];
    char *pc = c;
```

```
/* or char *pc = &c[0]; */

    sub(c,pc);
}

sub(c1,c2)
char c1[],*c2;
{
    /* ... */
}
```

In the above example, the arguments to function `sub` are a `char` array and a pointer to a `char`. As mentioned earlier, the array name `c` is actually interpreted as a pointer to that array (and therefore to `c[0]`), so both arguments are really pointers to `char`.

While the formal argument declarations in `sub` are correct they could also have been written as any one of the following.

```
            char c1[],c2[];
or          char *c1,*c2;
or          char *c1,c2[];
```

Variables with storage class `register` may be stored in actual machine registers. The number of variables actually stored in registers in each function is implementation-defined and the actual storage location of a `register` variable cannot be determined at run-time.

Even if a variable is stored in a register, that condition only exists throughout that function. If the variable is used as an argument to another function, there is no guarantee or requirement that it be declared with class `register` within that called function. Therefore, when a `register` variable is used as an actual argument, the `register` class is ignored.

Variables of any class can be used as actual arguments, but the class has no bearing on the way in which the argument list is set up.

```
/* funct3.c - passing register arguments */

main()
{
    register r1,r2,r3,r4;

    sub(r1,r2,r3,r4);
}

sub(r1,r2,r3,r4)
int r1,r2,r3,r4;
{
    /* ... */
}
```

Note that while r1, r2, r3, and r4 are all defined with class register in main, they are all declared as int in function sub. (Many compilers will only implement two or three register variables per function.) It is possible for a formal argument to have class register.

```
/* funct4.c - register formal arguments */

main()
{
    int i,j;

    sub(i,j);
}

sub(i,j)
int i;
register j;
{
    /* ... */
}
```

Here, argument j is defined as an int in main and as a register int in function sub. The formal argument list normally maps directly into the argument frame set up when the function was invoked. Therefore, the formal list does not usually take up any new storage space. It merely redefines space already allocated on the stack. One exception to this may occur when a formal argument is of class `register`.

If the compiler cannot or will not implement `j` in an actual register, then that class declaration is ignored and `j` continues to be used directly from the argument frame on the stack. If, however, a register is available for use, code is generated to copy `j` from the stack frame to that register. This allows loop counters and such to be placed in registers for faster processing.

Passing Variable Argument Lists

For certain applications it is useful to have a variable number of actual arguments. C does not support this capability directly, as the stack frame is not prefixed with an argument count. (Note that while some compilers, such as those on a DEC PDP-11 or VAX-11, may have access to the argument count, use of this feature would certainly be nonportable.)

If C doesn't support variable argument lists, then how does the `printf` function work? The first argument to `printf` always points to a string which may contain edit mask sequences beginning with a % character. By scanning this string, `printf` determines the number, type, and order of arguments that should follow the first one. Therefore, `printf` is really only interested in that first argument after which it must access the stack frame directly to get at any trailing arguments.

Obviously, `printf` must have an intimate knowledge of the structure of the stack frame (or whatever the argument passing mechanism happens to be) so that it can find and correctly interpret the arguments. For example, `printf` needs to know the size of each data type and any alignment considerations used to set up the argument list.

```
/* funct5.c - variable argument lists */

#include <stdio.h>

main()
{
    sub(3,-45,123,-543,89);
}

/* we intentionally specify only 1 arg for sub */

sub(i)
int i;
{
    int j,*pi;

    printf("arg #\taddress\tvalue\n");
    for (pi = &i,j = 0; j < 5; ++j,++pi) {
            printf("  %d\t%6u\t%4d\n",j,pi,*pi);
    }
}
```

arg #	address	value
0	3608	3
1	3610	-45
2	3612	123
3	3614	-543
4	3616	89

Function sub accesses all five arguments passed to it by using the address of the first argument and assuming that arguments are passed in the reverse order on the stack. However, the problem is that sub must know that five and only five arguments were passed and that each is an int. If more (or less) than five are used or their types are other than int, sub would not work correctly. This approach is very dependent on the compiler's specific argument passing mechanism and is therefore, nonportable.

Not only will this method differ from one system to the next, it may also vary between different compilers on the same system. The Intel 8088/86 family of processors support multiple-memory models, with which the size of pointers may vary from one model to the other. In this case, the argument stack frame must be interpreted differently for each model.

```
/* funct6.c — implementing the max function */

#include <stdio.h>

main()
{
    int i;

    i = imax(5,3,-45,123,-543,89);
    printf("The maximum value is %d\n",i);
    i = imax(3,-6,-4567,-23);
    printf("The maximum value is %d\n",i);
    i = imax(1,23456);
    printf("The maximum value is %d\n",i);
}

/* return the maximum of numarg integers */

imax(numarg)
int numarg;
{
    /* parg points to first int value */
    int *parg = (&numarg) + 1;
    register maximum = 0;

    if (numarg > 0) {
            maximum = *parg;
            while (--numarg) {
                    if (*(++parg) > maximum)
                            maximum = *parg;
            }
    }
    return (maximum);
}


The maximum value is 123
The maximum value is -6
The maximum value is 23456
```

Here, function `imax` returns the maximum of a given set of integer arguments. In order to handle a variable number of arguments, the count of integer values is passed as the first argument. To find the maximum of five values, six arguments are needed, the first of which contains the value '5'. Like `printf`, `imax` relies on the first argument being correct. If it is not, the wrong answer will most likely be returned.

For speed advantages, it might seem desirable to define `parg` as class `register`. However, on some implementations, such as the Intel Large Memory Model, a pointer is larger than a `register int`, in which case a pointer cannot be stored in a machine register. In this case any `register` class would be ignored although one would hope that the compiler would generate a warning message.

An alternate approach to passing an argument count is to terminate the argument list with some special value such as an integer zero (or a `'\0'` char). However, this will not work with `imax` as all possible integer values are valid inputs.

As a rule, variable argument processing should be reserved for those cases where there really isn't a better alternative.

Passing and Returning Structures

Newer compilers allow structures to be passed as arguments and returned as function values.

```
/* funct7.c - passing structure arguments */

#include <stdio.h>

struct st {
    int i;
    char c[6];
};

main()
{
    static struct st s = {26,"hello"};

    sub1(s);            /* call by value */
    sub2(&s);           /* call by address */
```

```
}

sub1(s)
struct st s;
{
    printf("i = %d, c = %s\n",s.i,s.c);
}

sub2(ps)
struct st *ps;
{
    printf("i = %d, c = %s\n",ps->i,ps->c);
}


i = 26, c = hello
i = 26, c = hello
```

Passing structures by value and by address is straightforward, however, there can be a problem when dealing with existing code. Compilers that do not support the passing of structures by value treat a structure argument as if its address were being used, not its value. So in the call `sub(s);`, where s is a structure, the address of s is passed, not its value. If this code is processed by a compiler that can pass structures by value, the function call would be incorrectly interpreted and the code will need to be changed to `sub(&s);`.

If you really mean to pass a structure by address, always use the & address-of prefix regardless of whether or not your compiler supports structure value arguments. (It is possible that an older compiler may reject such a construct or flag it as a warning.)

The following example shows how to return a structure and a pointer to a structure of the same type.

```
/* funct8.c - returning structures by value
            and by pointer */

struct st {
    int i;
    char c[6];
};

struct st sub1()
{
    static struct st s1 = {12,"abc"};

    return (s1);
}

struct st *sub2()
{
    static struct st s2 = {43,"xyz"};

    return (&s2);
}
```

Program Startup and Function main

C has no way of distinguishing a main program from its support routines, so a mechanism is needed to determine the program's entry point, hence the special function name main. Each C program that runs in a hosted environment (that is, one with an operating system) must have one and only one function defined with the name main.

Function main is only the conceptual entry point, it is not the actual place where the program module begins executing. When a C program's modules are linked together, a special startup object module is also needed. (A compiler may generate code such that this module is automatically included at link-time. See Chapter 6 for more details.)

This startup module has several functions. It processes the command-line and sets up the argc and argv (and possibly envp) arguments for main, it opens the files stdin, stdout, and stderr, it sets up stack and heap work space, and eventually transfers control to function `main` via a subroutine call.

The latter task means that when function `main` exits via a `return` statement or falls into its closing brace, control is passed back to the startup module which in turn may perform some cleanup, including passing any returned value back to the operating system's command-line processor. (Note that calling the `exit` function will generally cause control to be transferred to this startup routine directly.)

```c
/* funct9.c — function main */

#include <stdio.h>

extern int main(argc,argv)
int argc;
char *argv[];
{
    int i;

    for (i = 0; i < argc; ++i)
            printf("arg #%d = >%s<\n",i,argv[i]);
}


Using a command—line of:

program lower UPPER "sp ace" "t<tab>ab"

generates

arg #0 = ><
arg #1 = >lower<
arg #2 = >UPPER<
arg #3 = >sp ace<
arg #4 = >t            ab<
```

The program's command-line may be processed differently by different compilers and/or operating systems. Some environments may not recognize both upper- and lower-case or quoted literals. In the latter case, this means that command-line arguments cannot contain leading, trailing, or embedded white-space. On some systems (such as early versions of MS/PC-DOS), the program loader does not store the name of the program being run resulting in `argv[0]` pointing to a null (or some other implementation-defined) string. The `printf` function writes to the file `stdout`, which has been opened for output by the startup module.

Systems such as UNIX and MS/PC-DOS allow command-line redirection of `stdin` and `stdout` using < and > (or >>) respectively. This redirection is handled by the command-line processor itself and these characters and their associated file names and any '|' pipe characters are removed from the command-line before being passed to the startup module of the C program.

Systems that do not support this redirection facility directly can implement it in the compiler supplied program startup module. In this case, the <, >, and >> characters are passed as part of the command-line, and the startup module must take care of the file redirection itself.

The `void` Function Type

It is quite legitimate for a function to have no return value. In this case the function has no type and uses `return;` (or simply drops through the closing `}`) instead of `return (rvalue);`. Earlier compilers have no way of defining a function to be without type so a type of `int` (the default type) was recommended for this purpose and was generally implemented using

```
#define void int

void funct()
{
    /* ... */
    return;
}
```

While this documents the intent to have a typeless function, it provides no protection against a value accidentally being returned. Newer compilers implement a `void` function type directly using the `void` keyword. In this case, any function declared as `void` may not return a value or have its return value used in an expression.

```
/* funct10.c - the void function type */

main()
{
    void sub();

    sub();
}

void sub()
{
    /* ... */

    return;
}
```

In `funct10.c` above, it is illegal to have a statement such as `i = sub();` in `main`, as `sub` does not have a return value. A statement of `return (rvalue);` in function `sub` would also be flagged as an error.

Expression Evaluation Order

C makes no guarantee about the order of evaluation of expressions. In the expression (a + b) + c, the compiler is free to ignore the parentheses and to evaluate the expression as a + (b + c) instead. The impact of this is twofold.

```
/* funct11.c — expression evaluation order */

#include <stdio.h>

main()
{
    int i;

    i = f() + g() + h();
}

f()
{
    puts("In function f.");
    return (1);
}

g()
{
    puts("In function g.");
    return (2);
}

h()
{
    puts("In function h.");
    return (3);
}

One possible outcome might be

In function h.
In function g.
In function f.
```

First, the order of evaluation may change from one compiler to the next and it cannot be guaranteed between different releases of the same compiler or even between similar expressions within the same program. In the example above the functions f, g, and h just happen to be called in the reverse order of their reference.

Second, the order of evaluation of expressions within actual argument lists is not necessarily predictable.

```
f1(i,i++);
f2(j++ * j);
```

In this example, i++ may be evaluated before i and j may be evaluated before j++.

Miscellaneous Points

Some languages (or implementations of them) allow arguments in subroutine calls to be optional, in which case a default value is supplied by the called routine. They typically do this by just omitting the actual argument as follows.

```
/* funct12.c – optional function arguments */

main()
{
    int arg1,arg2,argn;

    sub(arg1,arg2, ,argn);
}
```

Here the third argument to sub has been omitted. C does not allow this and provides no other way to make leading or embedded arguments optional. (Trailing arguments can be omitted as discussed in Passing Variable Argument Lists above.) This forces the calling function to know exactly what the default value is if no value is supplied.

C allows functions without arguments in which case the actual argument list is empty. However, the parentheses are still required. While this may seem unnecessary, it does make the function call unambiguous as shown below.

```
/* functl3.c — functions without arguments */

main()
{
    double subd();
    double d;

    d = subd();
}
```

The parentheses in the declaration and use of subd leave no doubt that subd is indeed a function. However, some languages (in particular FORTRAN) have a problem with this construct.

```
version #1 — doesn't work as expected

    PROGRAM MAIN

    REAL*8 SUBD,D

    D = SUBD
    END
```

FORTRAN has no way to explicitly declare that SUBD is a function, so the code above treats SUBD as if it were a double precision variable rather than a function call.

```
version #2 - compilation error

     PROGRAM MAIN

     REAL*8 SUBD,D

     D = SUBD()
     END
```

By adding the parentheses to the function call, SUBD has explicitly been identified as a function, but unfortunately this will be flagged as an error by many compilers as a function must have at least one argument.

```
version #3 - works with fake argument

     PROGRAM MAIN

     REAL*8 SUBD,D

     D = SUBD(0)
     END

     SUBROUTINE SUBD(DUMMY)

     REAL*8 SUBD
     INTEGER*2 DUMMY

     SUBD = expression
     RETURN
     END
```

So, to get SUBD recognized as a function it must be given a fake argument so that the parentheses can be used in the call.

Why is this of interest to the C programmer? A number of the capabilities or requirements in C programs may seem unnecessary or messy, but if one looks at the problems suffered by older languages, one can begin to understand the reason for their presence in C. It has often been suggested that C was designed to make it easy to parse programs, and compared with most popular (and ambiguous) languages, it most certainly is.

By default, scalars are passed by value and aggregates are passed by address. If a called function is to legitimately update the value of any variable passed to it, that variable's address must be passed, not its value.

```
/* funct14.c - passing by value vs address */

#include <stdio.h>

main()
{
    int i = 5;

    power2(i);
    printf("i = %d\n",i);

    power2a(&i);
    printf("i = %d\n",i);
}

power2(i)
int i;
{
    i *= i;
}

power2a(pi)
int *pi;
{
    *pi *= *pi;
}


i = 5
i = 25
```

Function `power2` can only update its private copy of `i` (which is stored in the argument frame on the stack). It cannot affect the actual value of the variable passed to it. Function `power2a` on the other hand is passed the address of an integer and can therefore update it. (Passing an address instead a value is a problem commonly encountered when using the library routine `scanf`.)

Some implementations of FORTRAN always pass by address, so that in the statement CALL SUB(5), the address of the constant '5' is passed and if subroutine SUB modifies this value, the constant '5' will now have that new value instead of '5', meaning that constants may not always have a constant value. Fortunately, C does not suffer from this problem.

The choice of data types in C is usually made based on the intended purpose of the variable in question and the availability of certain kinds of storage (i.e., `static`, stack, and heap). The following program shows how `extern` storage class may be forced on a variable even it if is not required or desired. This program will give the results shown if the functions `sub1` and `sub2` are not overlaid against each other, but it may not if they are overlaid.

```
/* functl5.c - externals vs internal statics */

#include <stdio.h>

int excount = 0;

main()
{
    int i;

    for (i = 1; i <= 5; ++i) {
            subl();
            sub2();
    }
}

subl()
{
    /* some code which doesn't use excount */
}

sub2()
{
    extern int excount;
    static int iscount = 0;

    ++excount;
    ++iscount;
    printf("excount = %d\tiscount = %d\n",
            excount,iscount);
}


excount = 1       iscount = 1
excount = 2       iscount = 2
excount = 3       iscount = 3
excount = 4       iscount = 4
excount = 5       iscount = 5
```

Some fixed memory operating systems (such as RSX and RSTS on DEC PDP-11s) allow object modules within a program to be overlayed against each other so that the task's run-time address space can be kept within some limit (such as 64KB).

Consider an environment such as this, where two functions f1 and f2 overlay each other in memory and that both have internal `static` data variables defined. The overlay tree branch containing f1 is called a number of times and one or more of its `static`s is updated. The branch containing f2 is loaded over top of f1. When f1 is reloaded from disk again, what is the value of f1's `static`s? Do they contain the values last placed in them? One would hope so, but depending on how the `static` data area is organized by the compiler, the `static`s may be reinitialized to their compile-time values, in which case they would be wrong.

To get around this problem FORTRAN programmers are forced to create a dummy COMMON block, place these "local" variables in it, and to declare that COMMON in the main program (or at least at the appropriate part of the overlay tree) to ensure that these variable values will be preserved across overlay loads. C programmers, on the other hand, don't have COMMON blocks and have to resort to giving these variables `extern` class so they become part of the overlay tree root.

C's argument widening rules cause arguments of type `char`, `short`, and `float` to be converted to `int`, `int`, and `double`, respectively, so does it make sense to use them?

```
/* funct16.c - char, short and float usage */

#include <stdio.h>

main()
{
    char sub();
    char crval;
    char c = 'A';
    short s = 12;
    float f = 123.45;

    crval = sub(c,s,f);
    printf("c = %c, %d (dec)\n",crval,crval);
}

char sub(c,s,f)
char c;
short s;
float f;
{
    return (c + s);
}


c = M, 77 (dec)
```

There is no reason not to use these argument types because they appropriately reflect the variable type actually needed. Whether or not these variables are converted to another type during the function call is of no consequence to the programmer provided both the calling and the called function declare the argument in the same way and both actually refer to the same value (or address) in the argument list.

C's widening rules do *not* apply to return values. A function may have a return type of char, short, or float in which case such return values are not widened to int, int, and double as for function arguments.

It is quite common to ignore the value returned by a function. (How many programs check the return value from each printf call?) Return values are usually returned in one or more registers rather than on the stack, in which case, the return value can be ignored without any catastrophic consequences

96

at least on behalf of the compiler. Such actions can, however, cause problems at run-time, as the return values most often ignored are error codes from library functions such as `printf`, `puts`, `putchar` and `fclose`.

```
/* funct17.c — ignoring return values */

#include <stdio.h>

main()
{
    int printf();

    printf("Hello there.\n");
}
```

Ignoring return values in other than trivial test programs is not recommended. Functions that return values do so for a purpose, to let you know of the outcome of some particular process. If the value is worth returning, it's worth looking at. The values returned by the I/O library functions listed above (and others) are best processed by a general-purpose error-handling routine as follows.

```
void errproc();

errproc("main",printf(".....",...));
errproc("sub1",puts("hello there"));
```

It is necessary to restrict the choice of names for `extern` functions if the linker has limits on the length of external names that it can recognize. The linker may also be case-insensitive, so it is recommended that function names not contain upper-case letters. Also ensure that the first 6 characters of external names are unique. Some linkers (and object module librarians) may not be able to handle underscores in external names, which may further restrict the format of function names.

Some operating system libraries (such as DEC's VAX/VMS) have entry points that contain characters not allowed by C. (The $ symbol is particu-

97

larly common.) In these cases, the C compiler used must be modified to allow external function name references that contain these special characters. These calls should be clearly identified and isolated if portability is of concern.

Strictly speaking, `static` function names should not be seen by the linker, but compilers that do not implement this function class treat `static` functions as `extern` functions anyway.

The maximum number of arguments allowed in a function call is implementation-defined.

C allows recursion, so a function may invoke itself directly or indirectly. Since `main` is just "another C function" it can be recursively invoked, although it is hard to imagine a realistic example.

Pointers to Functions

To most high-level language programmers, pointers to functions in C remain a mystery, but the fact remains that they may save considerable coding and time in certain circumstances. Therefore, an understanding of them may prove useful.

Definition

Before looking at a useful application of function pointers, it is worth spending time to show exactly how pointers to functions can be defined and used.

```
/* ptrfunl.c - introduction to ptrs to functions */

#include <stdio.h>

main()
{
    char *mask,*str1,*str2;

    mask = "string 1 = %s string 2 = %s\n";
    str1 = "Monday";
    str2 = "December";
```

```
    printf(mask,str1,str2);

    sub(printf,mask,str1,str2);
}

sub(funct,mask,str1,str2)
int (*funct)();
char *mask,*str1,*str2;
{
    (*funct)(mask,str1,str2);
}


string 1 = Monday string 2 = December
string 1 = Monday string 2 = December
```

The call to function `sub` in `main` uses the function name `printf` as its first argument. Because `printf` has already been used as a function in the previous statement, the compiler knows how to generate the correct code for this argument, so it passes the address of the function `printf`. (Because functions can only be passed by address, the & operator is implied and need not be specified.) If the call to function `printf` is removed a compilation error something like

```
    sub(printf $$ ,mask,str1,str2);
    warning:undefined variable
```

should result which indicates that the object `printf` has not been declared. To resolve this problem `printf` must first be declared using

```
    . . .
    int printf();
    . . .
    sub(printf,mask,str1,str2);
    . . .
```

or by using #include <stdio.h> before the call to sub.

In function sub, the declaration int (*funct)(); indicates that the argument funct is a pointer to a function which returns an integer. (Note the difference between this declaration and int *funct() which indicates that funct is a function that returns a pointer to an integer.)

Because funct is a pointer to a function, (*funct) means "take the contents of the pointer funct" just as it would for any other type of pointer. The contents of the address pointed to by funct is the executable code of the function itself, so (*funct) translates to "call the function pointed to by funct." Therefore, the statement

```
(*funct)(mask,str1,str2);
```

has the same affect as

```
printf(mask,str1,str2);
```

and as shown, both produce the same output.

Transaction Processing

OK. Enough regurgitation. It's time to look at a realistic example. Suppose a program is to handle a number of different transaction or record types in the range 1 through 20, and that as each transaction arrives it is to be processed by a record type-specific function. The traditional way of handling this is by using a monstrous if/else or case construct as follows.

```
/* if/else version */

if (rectype == 1)
    procrt1();
else if (rectype == 2)
```

```
        procrt2();

    . . .

    else if (rectype == n)
        procrtn();

    /* switch version */

    switch (rectype) {

    case 1:
        procrt1();
        break;

    case 2:
        procrt2();
        break;

    . . .

    case n:
        procrtn();
        break;
```

Assembly language programmers might say "Why not have a table of function names that can be indexed by transaction type? This way, the driving program can be oblivious to the type of the transaction received and the corresponding processing function will be invoked much quicker than if a `switch` or `if/else` construct were used." Such a table is commonly used in assembly language programming and is often referred to as a "jump table".

The following example assumes three possible transaction types, namely 0, 1, and 2 whose corresponding processing functions are `sub0`, `sub1`, and `sub2`.

```
/* ptrfun2.c - storing function ptrs in an array */

#include <stdio.h>

main()
{
    int i;                    /* index variable */
    int sub0(),sub1(),sub2();/* declare function types */
    int (*funct)();           /* single function ptr */
    int (*funptr[3])();       /* array of function ptrs */

    funct = sub0;             /* point to function sub0 */
    (*funct)();               /* call sub0 */

    funptr[0] = sub0;          /* setup ptr array */
    funptr[1] = sub1;
    funptr[2] = sub2;

    for (i = 0; i < 3; ++i)    /* call sub0, sub1, sub2 */
            (*funptr[i])();
}

sub0()
{
    printf("Inside function sub0\n");
}

sub1()
{
    printf("Inside function sub1\n");
}

sub2()
{
    printf("Inside function sub2\n");
}


Inside function sub0
Inside function sub0
Inside function sub1
Inside function sub2
```

The statement `funct = sub0;` assigns the address of function `sub0` to `funct` and once again `sub0` is invoked indirectly using `(*funct)();`. Note that if `sub0` were not declared, `funct = sub0;` would cause `sub0` to be flagged by the compiler as an undefined object. Because functions `sub0`, `sub1` and `sub2` must be explicitly declared in `main` they must be given a return type, in this case, `int`. Even though these functions do not return a value, they must have a type to satisfy the language declaration syntax requirements. Of course, if such a function returned a value of type other than `int`, the appropriate type should be used instead. (If your compiler supports the `void` function type and a function does not return a value, that function should be declared to be of type `void`.)

The declaration `int (*funptr[3])();` indicates that `funptr` is an array of three pointers to functions which return integers, while the statement `funptr[0] = sub0;` assigns the address of function `sub0` to the first array element. Because `funptr` is an array, its elements can be referenced by subscript, such as in `(*funptr[i])();` which invokes the function pointed to by element i. And, hey, presto! We have an array of function names that can be called by knowing the array index (which, for this example is a transaction type).

```
/* ptrfun3.c - initializing an array of function ptrs */

#include <stdio.h>

main()
{
    int i;                      /* index variable */
    int sub0(),sub1(),sub2();   /* declare function types */
    static int (*funptr[3])()   /* array of function ptrs */
            = {sub0,sub1,sub2};

    for (i = 0; i < 3; ++i)  /* call sub0, sub1, sub3 */
        (*funptr[i])();
}


Inside function sub0
Inside function sub1
Inside function sub2
```

Example `ptrfun2.c` defines the function pointer table at run-time, a rather expensive approach considering that the function names and their order in the table will most likely remain constant throughout the program. Example `ptrfun3.c` shows how to define the table as a `static`, local array, using

```
static int (*funptr[3])() = {sub0,sub1,sub2};
```

This definition and initialization is similar to that for any other array. Note, however, that the function names must not be in quotation marks and that they must have been explicitly declared or invoked prior to this statement so that they are correctly recognized as functions.

```
/* ptrfun4.c - more on initializing an array
              of function ptrs. */

#include <stdio.h>

int sub0(),sub1(),sub2();
int (*funptr[3])() = {sub0,sub1,sub2};

main()
{
    int i;

    for (i = 0; i < 3; ++i)
            (*funptr[i])();
}
```

This example is very similar to `ptrfun3.c` except that the pointer name table is global. Note again that the functions referenced in the initialization must have been declared previously.

The Mechanics

"Just what exactly is a pointer to a function and when is it known?" Perhaps that's best explained by looking at the Intel 8088/86 code generated by the relevant parts of `ptrfun1.c`, above (which uses the S model — small program and small data). The function pointer code generated by the compiler is based on the offset of the function from a particular base address, neither of which is known at compile-time. The actual addresses of these are resolved at link-time when the function is finally assigned an actual starting address relative to the executable module's base or other segment.

```
. . .
printf(mask,strl,str2);
sub(printf,mask,strl,str2);            /* pass ptr to printf */

    PUBLIC printf_
    PUBLIC sub_

main_:      PUSH BP
    . . .
    MOV AX,OFFSET printf_   /* get adr of printf */
    PUSH AX
    CALL sub_               /* call sub */
    . . .
    POP BP
    RET

sub(funct,mask,strl,str2)
int (*funct)();
char *mask,*strl,*str2;
{
    (*funct)(mask,strl,str2);

sub_: PUSH BP
    MOV BP,SP
    PUSH WORD [BP+10]       /* push str2 arg */
    PUSH WORD [BP+8]        /* push strl arg */
    PUSH WORD [BP+6]        /* push mask arg */
    CALL WORD [BP+4]        /* call function
                            pointed to by funct */
    MOV SP,BP
    POP BP
    RET
    END
```

Once an executable module is linked, all functions have been assigned starting addresses and function pointers can now take on actual values. While
the actual address contained in a pointer to a function is probably meaningless (and one should certainly not rely on that value), you may want to look
at it using the following program.

```
/* ptrfun5.c - displaying a function's address */

#include <stdio.h>

main()
{
    int printf();

    sub(printf);
}

sub(funct)
int (*funct)();
{
    (*funct)("The address of printf = %u\n",funct);
}
```

The second argument to the function call in sub MUST be funct, not
*funct. If *funct were used instead, it would cause the printf function
to be invoked again, and this time without any arguments.

Note that displaying a pointer as an unsigned int is inherently nonportable, and depending on your compiler's pointer size, you may need to use
%lu instead (as in the Intel 8086 Large Memory model). In any case, pointer
values are not meant to be displayed.

An interesting problem arises on 8086 machines, where the following four
memory models can be used.

Model	Code size	Data size	Size of code address	Size of data address
Small	64KB	64KB	2 bytes	2 bytes
Data	64KB	1MB	2	4
Program	1MB	64KB	4	2
Large	1MB	1MB	4	4

For simplicity, it is desirable for pointers to data and pointers to functions to be the same size in the program. This is automatically true for the S and L models where all pointers are 2 and 4 bytes respectively. In the D model, data addresses are 4 bytes, while all code addresses can be represented in 2 bytes. To make these the same size, a zero-filled high-order word is added to all function pointer addresses.

The P model is quite different as all data pointers are 2 bytes, while function pointers require 4-byte addresses. If all data pointers are extended to 32 bits by adding a zero high-order word, this would defeat the purpose of using the P model instead of the L model. So rather than extend all data pointers (which are more common than function pointers), function pointers are forced to be accessed via 16 bits. This requires the use of a 16-bit "pseudo-function pointer", which points to a 32-bit address in the data segment, which in turn contains the real address of the function. Hence, for this model, the address contained by a function pointer is *not* the address of the function; it is a pointer to the address of the function.

Changing Function Pointers at Run-Time

The above discussion has been limited to static lists of function pointers but as these pointers are variables, their values can be changed at run-time. By using this knowledge, one function could be substituted for another at run-time. For example, in an application, a user is gathering frequencies of the occurrences of certain values. Sometimes they want an average of all possible value occurrences and sometimes they just want an average of all the values for which there was at least one occurrence. Assuming these averages are calculated by the functions average and naverage, respectively, this program can be written as follows.

```
/* ptrfun6.c - changing function pointers */

main()
{
    int i;
    int average(), naverage();
    int (*funptr)() = average;

    /* get user direction as to which
       function to use */

    i = getfun();
```

```
        if (i == 'A')
                funptr = average;
        else
                funptr = naverage;

        (*funptr)(arg-list);
}
```

By displaying the possible alternatives for a calculation on a menu, the user could select the required option, which would in turn cause the corresponding function to be used. By initializing the pointer to point to the function `average`, that function becomes the default method for calculating the average unless it is overridden by the user at run-time. If for some reason, an average should not or cannot be calculated during a particular part of the program, the function pointer could be set to zero to indicate this. This method can also be used as a stub for options that appear on the menu but are not yet implemented.

Some Limitations

The above examples work well in a situation where all transaction processing functions have no arguments, have exactly the same arguments, or use externals for interfunction linkage. Unfortunately, this is not always always the case if something like

```
        int suba(),subb(),subc();
        int i;
        char c;
        char *pc;

        suba();
        subb(i,c);
        subc(i,c,pc);
```

is required. Here, each of the functions requires a different number (and type) of arguments and so a generic call, such as

```
(*funptr[i])(arg1,arg2,...,argn);
```

to all of these functions is impossible. Unfortunately, we must revert back to an if/else or case construct, unless we want to use externals instead of argument passing. While using externals obscures the data-linkage process, if designed properly and documented thoroughly, it still allows the power of function pointers to be used and in a transaction processing environment, the extra speed gained by not having to set up and clean up the argument stack frame may make all the difference.

It may be possible to handle a variable type and size argument list by using a complicated union and structure arrangement. In the simplest form, where each function has one argument but each argument has a different type, a union of each possible type could be constructed. Then, a pointer to that union could be passed as an argument.

The earlier examples also rely on the fact that all service functions return values of the same type, and again, this may not be the case. The declaration of int (*funptr[3])(); allows an incoming transaction type to be used as a subscript into the array funptr, but it requires that each function return an int. Consider the following case.

```
int subx();
int *suby();
double *subz();
```

Again, there is no easy way to write a general function call because we can no longer use an array of function pointers and we cannot use one variable to hold an object of each returned type. The array problem could possibly be circumvented by using an array of pointers to pointers to functions where each function pointer is explicitly cast into some generic pointer type and stored in another array. However, this messy process still doesn't solve the returned value problem and once again it's back to the if/else and case alternatives.

It might be possible to handle multiple return types by having each function return a pointer to a union of all possible types, although this approach would not allow the use of void function types.

One final comment about pointers to functions. Their usage does *not* help to document source code. One cannot look at source code and tell exactly which function is being invoked if a pointer to function is being used. Likewise, the output from a cross-reference utility cannot include such function names, as they are only known at run-time.

Pointers to functions need not be complicated. While their use may be prohibited by the above-mentioned (or other) limitations, for certain applications, they can provide simpler (and possibly faster) transaction processing code.

The X3J11 Draft

A number of function-related aspects are changed or introduced in the proposed ANSI Standard. They are:

- Function prototypes - These allow a dummy definition of a function call to be declared along with argument types so that the argument list in a calling function can be matched against that expected by the called function. Prototypes also allow `char`, `short`, and `float` arguments to be passed as such without being widened to `int`, `int`, and `double` respectively.

- A `stdarg.h` header file and several macro definitions allow the definition and use of variable argument lists in a portable fashion.

- Structures and unions may be passed by value as well as by address.

- The `void` data type can be applied to functions only and functions of type `void` may not return a value or have their "returned" value used.

- To strictly conform to the Standard, `main` must be defined as `extern int main(argc,argv)` or `extern int main()`. The prefix `extern int` is the default class and type for a function.

- At least thirty-one arguments are allowed in a function call.

- Refer to the end of Chapter 6 for a discussion of command-line processing and `main`'s arguments `argc` and `argv`.

- All library functions must be declared in the appropriate standard headers; even those functions returning an `int` value.

- Function prototypes are discussed in detail in Chapter 7.

CHAPTER 4

Data Storage—The Stack and Heap

The C language offers considerably more options for data typing and space allocation than do most other commonly used languages. This seems reasonable considering C's role as a systems language. However, these options are not available free of charge. They involve the familiar speed versus storage tradeoff and their usage can require more than a superficial understanding.

The main temporary data storage areas used by C are the stack and the heap. A programmer can write significant amounts of reasonable code without an intimate understanding of these two concepts. However, to take full advantage of C's storage class mechanisms (and possibly to get some programs to run), one must be aware of the inner workings of the stack. (The material in this chapter assumes that your implementation actually uses a stack mechanism for temporary variable storage and argument passing.)

The way in which the stack is implemented may vary considerably from one compiler to the next so implementation-specific details will be omitted. Instead, the discussion will focus on the ways in which these storage areas might be used by the programmer and the compiler itself. Also suggestions will be made that may result in more effective use of the stack.

Introduction

The stack is an area of memory set aside for temporary storage. It is managed on a LIFO (last in/first out) basis, so values are retrieved (popped) from the stack in the reverse order in which they were stored (pushed). Modern operating systems typically set up and maintain a special hardware stack whose status is monitored by a special hardware register called the Stack Pointer (SP).

C compilers running on these systems usually use this stack to store automatic variables, to facilitate function linkage, and to store compiler-generated temporary variables. (Software stacks may also be set up by the programmer within a C program, however, these stacks are not accessible by the C compiler and their usage will not be covered in this chapter.)

Why are we interested in C's stack mechanism anyway? First, the more that is understood about the stack, the more effectively it can be used. Second, on many systems, the amount of memory allocated to the stack is fixed at program link- or load-time. Therefore, precautions must be taken to ensure that the program does not try to use more stack space than it has. (Virtual memory operating systems typically allow a stack's upper limit to change dynamically as needed at run-time and consequently don't suffer from stack overflow problems.)

While programs (written in any high-level language) that run on a fixed-memory operating system are generally subject to stack size limitations, those written in C require even more consideration because of the existence of automatic variables. Space for automatic variables is typically allocated on the stack. Automatic variables can be defined at the start of any block (compound statement) and if a particular block is not executed, no stack space need be allocated for its variables. Therefore, the amount of stack space required for automatic variable storage depends entirely on the logic flow of the program, which in turn is dependent on the actual data being processed. And this data may vary from one program execution to the next. The trick then, is to have a sufficiently large enough stack for *each* program execution, without being unnecessarily wasteful.

Some systems have a maximum stack size. (8-bit and 16-bit systems might allow a maximum stack size of 64KB, for example.) So not only are a program's stack requirements important it is also necessary to ensure that these requirements don't exceed the space available. Even though a system may allow a given amount of stack space to be addressed, less physical memory may be available. Stack size may be limited by physical or cost considerations rather than CPU addressability. (This problem usually occurs in embedded systems such as those used in process control and instrumentation.)

Apart from the possibility of needing to keep within some maximum stack size, it may also be desirable to limit stack usage for speed or other reasons. In any case, the amount of temporary data space needed by a program should be analyzed during the design phase. In C, data can be created dy-

114

namically on the stack or the heap, or it can be statically allocated in a permanent data segment at compile-time. The maximum size of each of these storage areas, the frequency of variable use, and the lifetime and scope of variables should all be considered when deciding exactly which storage class to use for each particular variable.

If you neglect to consider these data space requirements during the design process, you may finish up with a perfectly good program that in theory will run, but due to excessive data space requirements cannot be compiled or linked or run without error. In many ways, this whole problem is similar to that of object module overlaying on fixed-memory systems.

Automatic Variables

Space for automatic variables is generally reserved by adjusting the stack pointer rather than by pushing zero or some other known value onto the stack a number of times. C makes no guarantee about the initial value of automatic variables, so you should explicitly initialize them if they need to contain a predictable value.

Consider the following set of automatic variable definitions.

```
/* stackl.c - auto storage allocation */

sub()
{
    char c1,c2;
    short s;
    int i;
    long l;
    unsigned u;
    float f;
    double d;
}
```

On a DEC PDP-11 (a 16-bit machine), 24 bytes are reserved on the stack for the eight automatic variables; one for each char, two each for short, int, and unsigned, four each for long and float and eight for double. On a DEC VAX (a 32-bit machine), 28 bytes are reserved, with two extra each for the long and unsigned variables. When function sub terminates, this storage space is released by adjusting the stack pointer to its value on input. If the declaration for the char variable c2 is omitted on a PDP system, the compiler still reserves 24 bytes. That is, it forces word (even byte) alignment on the stack starting with variable s to avoid our old friend, the Odd Address Trap (generated when a word operation is attempted on an odd address boundary).

A number of machines, such as the PDP-11, have certain data alignment requirements. Other machines, such as the VAX and Intel 8086-based systems, don't require such alignment but they can give better performance for some operations (such as memory fetches) if certain boundary alignments are followed. Good optimizing compilers for these machines may leave holes on the stack in order to get better alignment. As a result, a set of auto definitions may take up considerably more stack space than you think. If your compiler generates assembler source, it might be of interest to inspect the compiler's stack management ability.

Optimizing auto Definitions

If your compiler actually allocates stack space to variables in exactly the same order that they are defined, you may be able to help save stack space by specifying the definitions in decreasing order of alignment requirement. This will be particularly true for systems that require or can benefit from specific variable alignment.

The following example shows such an ordering. If auto structures and unions are defined, you will need to find out their alignment requirements so they can be given the appropriate ranking.

```
/* stack2.c - auto definition order */

sub()
{
    double d;
    float f;
    long l;
    unsigned u;
    int i;
    short s;
    char c1,c2;
}
```

Smarter compilers will rearrange the defined variable order anyway, totally ignoring any order you have used, so they can implement their own optimized ordering. Other, not-so-smart compilers just plain change the order for no obvious good reason.

If your ordering helps generate better stack usage, you have gained. If not, you haven't lost anything. In any case, the recommended ordering process can greatly enhance program readability (and hence maintainability). By defining all variables of the same type together in decreasing type order of alignment and alphabetically by name within type, it becomes a simple task to locate variable definitions within any block. Placing each variable on its own line along with a comment helps even more, particularly when cutting and pasting in a text editor.

Overlaying auto **Data**

Consider the case of a program that has three phases, each of which uses a large amount of stack space for auto variable storage. If each phase is executed serially, then at most only one set of auto variables need be in existence at any one time.

```
/* stack3.c - overlaying of auto data */

main()
{
    char c[1000];

    initial();
    process();
    cleanup();

    /* ... */
}

initial()
{
    char sc1[1000];

    /* ... */
}

process()
{
    char sc2[500];

    /* ... */
}

cleanup()
{
    char sc3[1200];

    /* ... */
}
```

The 1000 bytes of stack used by c in main remain allocated throughout the life of the program. However, as functions initial, process, and cleanup are mutually exclusive, they can share the same stack space for their auto variables sc1, sc2, and sc3. Therefore, the maximum amount of stack they need is 1200 bytes (ignoring stack management overhead). This gives a total stack requirement of 2200 bytes (1000 for c and a maximum of 1200 for sc3). If all three service functions were part of main, the total requirement would be 3700 bytes, as all auto variables would exist simultaneously.

Automatic variables can be defined at the start of any block (compound statement) so there can be a hierarchical nested structure of such variables within a function as shown by the following example. It may therefore be tempting to expect auto data between blocks at the same level to be overlayed as seen above with functions at the same level.

```
/* stack4.c - data overlaying within a function */

main()
{
    char ch[100];

    /* ... */

    if (ch[0] == 'A') {
            char a[100];

            /* ... */
    }
    else if (ch[0] == 'B') {
            char b[200];

            /* ... */
    }
    else {
            char c[150];
            int i;

            /* ... */

            if (i == 0) {
                    int j[20];

                    /* ... */
            }
            else {
                    int k[10];

                    /* ... */
            }
    }
}
```

Variables a, b, and c are all defined at the same block level and so it might be expected that they share the same stack space. Likewise for j and k. In actual fact, this does not occur, because space for all auto variables within a function is typically allocated as soon as that function is entered. The reason for this will follow shortly. The above program actually behaves as if it were written as:

```
/* stack5.c - allocate all local data at once */

main()
{
    char ch[100];
    char a[100];
    char b[200];
    char c[150];
    int i;
    int j[20];
    int k[10];

    /* ... */

    if (ch[0] == 'A') {

            /* ... */
    }
    else if (ch[0] == 'B') {

            /* ... */
    }
    else {

            /* ... */

            if (i == 0) {

                    /* ... */
            }
            else {

                    /* ... */
            }
    }
}
```

Even though a compiler won't actually overlay `auto` data between blocks at the same level, there are compelling reasons to write code as indicated in `stack4.c`, above, rather than as shown in `stack5.c`. First, writing programs this way logically reflects what you really mean, and second, restricting the scope of local variables to only that needed will help to eliminate potential sources of error.

Using the example `stack5.c`, it is possible to eliminate variables a and c and to use b in place of all three, as a, b, and c are all `char` arrays of 200 bytes or less. Therefore, they don't need to exist at the same time so they can share stack space. While this would reduce the stack space required, one variable is being used for three different purposes depending on the state of the program and each interpretation uses a different amount of the array allocated. Not only can this be confusing, but if you are using a debugging tool that permits array bounds checking, it will be impossible to detect this type of error. For example, if a, b, and c are defined separately, a reference of a[110] would be flagged as illegal by such a tool. However, if the array b were used to implement a, b, and c then an erroneous reference to a[110] would go undetected.

Unraveling the Mystery

Earlier it was stated that compilers will not share stack space between `auto` variables at the same block level in a function. The reason is not obvious unless you have studied the seemingly innocuous `goto` statement and its effect on `auto` variables when one jumps into a subordinate block.

```
/* stack6.c — transferring into a block */

main()
{
    /* ... */

    goto label1;

    /* ... */

    goto label2;

    /* ... */

    {
```

```
            int i[10];

labell:                 ;              /* must have null stmt */

            /* ... */

label2:                 ;              /* must have null stmt */

            /* ... */
        }
}
```

Automatic variable definitions may contain initializing values. This initialization is guaranteed to happen *only* if their parent block is entered normally—by dropping into it from a higher level block. Using the goto statement and labels, it is possible to jump into the middle of a block as shown in the example above. If this is done, there is no guarantee that any auto initialization is done. (In fact, it is almost certain that it will not be done.) Regardless of whether or not auto variables are actually initialized, space will be allocated for them.

The real question is "Just when does stack space for the array i actually take place?" For any given block, it can be entered by falling into it or by any one of a (possibly) large number of labels throughout it. Regardless of the method of entry, the auto stack space must always be reserved (even if it isn't initialized). To do this, the compiler either has to allocate the space in a common and predictable place once only, or it has to generate code to allocate it at every possible entry point, at the same time ensuring that the allocation code at label2 is not executed if entry was made at labell. Obviously, the latter approach would require large amounts of very messy (and duplicated) code.

It seems then that the former solution is much easier to implement, but where is that common and predictable place? Because the actual entry point to the block is not known at compile-time, the common place must be outside of that block. Actually, the only place that can be guaranteed to have space allocated once and only once, such that this allocation is not run-time data dependent, is at the start of the function. Program stack4.c is therefore actually implemented as shown in stack5.c in the sense that all auto space for all blocks is allocated at the same time. Note, however, that the scope of each auto variable in stack4.c remains just within that variable's defining and subordinate blocks as expected.

One interesting note about the null statements used after the labels in the above example. A label must always be attached to a statement. It cannot simply be followed by a right brace. To satisfy this requirement, each label is followed with a null statement. (Actually only label2 need be followed by a null statement, as this would also satisfy label1's requirements.) This situation only occurs above because the example is unrealistic. In production programs, labels would typically be followed by actual statements.

Functions and the Stack

On stack-oriented machines, C compilers usually use the stack for inter-function linkage. Understanding how this linkage works allows programmers to interface with code written in other languages as well as to find out the amount of stack space used during function calls.

```
/* stack7.c - function argument passing */

main()
{
    int fp1;
    double fp2;
    register fp3;

    sub(fp1,fp2,fp3);
}
```

Function sub is invoked with three arguments. These arguments are pushed onto the stack in the reverse order of their specification. Variable fp3 is pushed first, followed by fp2 and fp1. This means that fp1 is on the top of the stack when sub begins executing. Knowing this order is particularly important when calling non-C routines from C. Although this argument ordering is fairly common with high-level languages, it is obviously necessary with printf whose calling sequence is

```
printf("edit mask",arg1,arg2...argn);
```

The first argument to printf dictates just how many other arguments (and their types) should be expected. Since printf allows a variable number of arguments, the first one must be located in a predictable place on the stack after printf gains control. If printf's arguments were passed to it in left-to-right order, printf would never be able to find the edit mask as the number of arguments passed on the stack is not known. Therefore, the arguments are pushed onto the stack in reverse order so that the address of the edit mask string is guaranteed to be the top argument.

(Note that an implementation is free to pass the number of arguments at the beginning of the stack frame or via a register if this is desirable and possible, in which case arguments could be passed from left to right.)

Since the storage size of C data types may vary from one implementation to the next, the stack space they require as function arguments varies accordingly. Note that fp3 is always passed on the stack even if it currently is stored in a machine register.

```
/* stack8.c - function formal arguments */

sub( fp1, fp2, fp3)
int fp1;
double fp2;
register fp3;
{
}
```

The formal arguments at the beginning of a function effectively define stack offsets into the existing argument list set up by the calling function. These formal arguments do not require stack space. If the compiler can honor the register class request, it generates code to copy fp3 from the stack into the appropriate hardware register. If this request cannot be honored, the fp3 value on the stack is used as is.

```
/* stack9.c - stack cleanup on return */

main()
{
    int ap1;
    double ap2;
    long ap3;

    int bp1;
    long bp2;

    suba(ap1,ap2,ap3);
    subb(bp1,bp2);
}

/* file suba.c */

suba(ap1,ap2)
int ap1;
double ap2;
{
    /* ... */
}

/* file subb.c */

subb(bp1,bp2,bp3)
int bp1;
long bp2;
double bp3;
{
    /* ... */
}
```

Each function is responsible for cleaning up the stack space allocated by it. When a function terminates, it must reclaim any stack space allocated to `auto` variables, and it typically does this by restoring the stack pointer to its original value on input to that function. When a function is called, the caller allocates stack space for the arguments. When the called function returns control, this stack space must also be released. This is important because it guarantees that exactly the same amount of space allocated is released.

Consider the case in which a function is called with more or fewer arguments than are actually expected, as shown above. Even though this is blatantly an error there is no mechanism within C to detect it. However, this erroneous code will not mess up the stack because stack space for the arguments is allocated and freed by the same function. If this were not the case, `main` would push three arguments on the stack and `suba` would only pop off two leaving the stack "off-by-1" during subsequent use, a situation that could not be tolerated.

When `auto` space is reserved on the stack, it is usually done by subtracting n from the stack pointer where n bytes (or words) is sufficiently large to hold all `auto` variables. Each `auto` variable is not pushed individually except for very primitive compilers such as early versions of small-C. Likewise, restoring the stack pointer when the function exits does not involve popping individual variables. Therefore, the amount of code that is generated to set up and clean up `auto` stack space is independent of the number of `auto` variables involved.

```
/* stackl0.c - argument type mismatch */

main()
{
    int pl,p2;

    subl(pl);
    sub2(pl,p2);
}

/* subl.c */

subl(pl)
long pl;
{
    /* ... */
}

/* sub2.c */

sub2(pl,p2)
long pl;
int p2;
{
    /* ... */
}
```

Formal arguments map into a stack frame that was created by the calling function and it is up to the programmer to make sure that the number, order, type, and size of the dummy arguments match those passed. If there is a mismatch, as shown above, the stack frame will be interpreted incorrectly, resulting in incorrect values being used.

Generally, the amount of stack space used for function calls is small compared to that used by auto variable allocation. Of course it could use more, particularly if there are large argument lists and/or small numbers of auto variables used. An increasing number of compilers also support the passing of structures (and unions) by value as well as address. When a structure (or union) is passed by value, the whole structure (or union) is pushed onto the stack. This means that a 100-byte structure requires 100 bytes of stack as an argument, whereas passing a pointer to that structure would only require (typically) 2 or 4 bytes. This difference is significant particularly if the function is called recursively.

Recursion and the Stack

Recursion is the process by which a function directly or indirectly invokes itself. The C language supports this notion and it has some interesting connotations. Realistically, if function fl calls itself recursively, this is no different from that function being called multiple times by some other function(s). Either way, it results in new auto storage space being allocated on the stack for each invocation.

```
/* stackll.c - recursion and the stack */

outdec(number)
int number;
{
    int val;

    if (number < 0) {
            putchar('-');
            number = -number;
    }
    if ((val = number/10) != 0)
            outdec(val);
    putchar((number % 10) + '0');
}
```

In the above example, outdec calls itself directly n times where n depends on the magnitude of the integer argument initially passed to it. Each time outdec is invoked by itself (or any other function), a new variable val is created on the stack. Obviously, if a function has 100 bytes of auto storage and it calls itself recursively to a depth of 10, then 1000 bytes of stack will be needed. The problem with this technique is that the amount of stack required depends entirely on the data being processed. So space must be allowed for the maximum possible requirements to avoid stack overflow. This problem may in fact dictate that recursion not be used.

The problem can be more acute if the recursive function passes structures (or unions) by value and these structures (or unions) are large.

129

Stack Overflow

Stack overflow must be avoided for the code to compile, link, and run properly. The C language provides no indication about stack requirements. In fact, it makes no comment about stacks at all. It is up to the implementer to decide how auto variables and argument passing are implemented. However, many implementations that use the stack approach do provide a mechanism to detect stack overflow at run-time. In the simplest form, they display a message to that effect on the user's terminal and abort the program. Better handlers may generate a software interrupt allowing the user program to regain control and possibly to take action to alleviate the problem.

Systems that implement stack overflow detection may allow this facility to be switched on and off. The theory is that this facility should be activated during testing and then, as it is expensive, it should be switched off in production code. Very few production programs are exhaustively tested due to time constraints or the huge number of possible logic flow paths so deactivation of this mechanism should only be done after considerable thought.

```
/* stackl2.c — stack overflow detection */

main()
{
    double d[30000];
}
```

On systems with only a 64KB stack, the above program will cause unpredictable behavior if stack overflow detection is nonexistent or disabled. Of course, this is an unrealistic and obvious situation. In reality, stack overflow situations are not quite so obvious.

Miscellaneous Stack Considerations

On systems designed to be stored in ROM (Read-Only Memory) extra care must be taken with stack usage because the stack may be the only RAM (writable memory) available to the program.

When a compiler generates code for complex expressions, it may create temporary, intermediate variables either in registers or on the stack. If the stack is used, the space required is entirely dependent on the complexity of the expression and its order of evaluation.

```
/* stack13.c - excess register variables */

sub()
{
    register r1,r2,r3,r4,r5,r6;
}
```

The register storage class is a hint to the compiler to use a hardware register to store a particular variable if possible. However, if this is not possible, the variable is treated as an auto and space for it is allocated on the stack. Without a close look at a compiler's generated code, the effects of register variable allocation on stack space is impossible to determine. However, one thing is reasonably certain. Most C compilers do not implement more than three or four register variables in any one function so register declarations in excess of these are likely to be treated as auto.

C makes no guarantee about the contents of uninitialized auto variables. It is possible that a particular implementation will allow the stack to be initialized to a given set of values at program link or load time. However, functions at the same level share stack space so this system stack initialization is only guaranteed to be in effect during the first branch of the program logic tree. After that, residual garbage will be left on the stack each time a lower-level function terminates.

When auto variable space is allocated, the required byte (or word) count is subtracted from the stack pointer. However, before this is done, the stack pointer must be saved somewhere (typically in a register) so that it can be restored properly when the function exits. The register used for this copy may already contain a value required later so that value must be saved before the copy is made and this is typically done by pushing it onto the stack. A possible scenario for stack set up and clean up is as follows.

```
f1()
{
    int a1,a2,a3;

    f2(a1,a2,a3);
}

f2(a1,a2,a3)
int a1,a2,a3;
{
}
```

1. Function f1 calls f2 with three arguments, resulting in each argument being pushed onto the stack along with f1's return address.

2. Function f2 pushes the value of a register on the stack and copies the Stack Pointer to it.

3. The Stack Pointer is then adjusted to allocate space for any auto variables.

4. If f2 calls other functions, it allocates and frees equal amounts of stack space as necessary.

5. If f2 used the stack for intermediate variable storage, it cleans this up as necessary.

6. Just before f2 terminates, it restores the stack pointer from the copy previously saved in the register in item 2, above, and restores the initial value of that register by popping it from the stack.

7. Function f2 then returns control to f1 popping off the return address and then f1 removes the argument list.

When all object modules of a C program are linked, a special startup module must be included. (It may automatically be included by the linker or it may need explicit mention in the link command. Refer to Chapter 6 for details.) This module handles command-line processing, opens the standard files and performs other initializing tasks before it transfers control to the user's `main` function. This code may use a significant amount of stack space depending on its functionality. At a minimum, it pushes the `argc` and `argv` arguments (and `envp`, if it exists) on the stack.

Function arguments are normally passed in the reverse order of their specification in the function call. This ordering cannot be optimized by the compiler as the calling and called functions may be compiled from separate source files. On systems where variable alignment is necessary or beneficial, there may be some advantage to ordering the argument list in decreasing alignment requirements for the same reasons discussed with `auto` variable ordering above. Such reordering may result in stack space savings.

The Heap

The heap is an area of memory that can be allocated and deallocated dynamically at run-time. Each program has its own heap. This scratch-pad pool is monitored by a heap manager that records allocated and free space addresses and lengths. This manager must handle deallocation and reallocation as well as handling space allocation.

As shown in `stack6.c`, all `auto` temporary data space is typically allocated each time a function is entered. Therefore, a function cannot decide whether to allocate space based on some event or data because either it has it reserved via an `auto` variable at compile-time or it doesn't. Frequently it is necessary to allocate space dynamically at run-time and obviously this cannot be done on the stack, at least not via `auto` variables.

Enter the heap. This block of memory is implemented separately from the stack although, the two may share the same data segment (and subsequently a combined upper size limit). While the size of the stack can usually be set by the programmer, the maximum size of the heap might be fixed. The heap might reside in address space unused by the program yet addressable by it. Therefore, the size of the heap may reduce proportionally as the size of the program code increases. In this case, as your program grows during development, you may be able to allocate less and less heap space.

The following example demonstrates the way in which the heap can be used.

133

```
/* heapl.c - allocate cleared dynamic array */

#include <stdio.h>

main()
{
    char *calloc();
    char *malloc();
    char *realloc();
    void free();

    int i;
    int *piarray;
    int *picopy;
    double *pdarray;
    float *pfarray;

    /* allocate a 10 element int array. It
       should be initialized to zero. */

    piarray = (int *) calloc(10,sizeof(int));

    if (piarray != NULL) {
            puts("\nint array allocated\n");
            puts("Initial contents are:\n");
            for (i = 0; i < 10; i++) {
                    printf("%2d ",piarray[i]);
                    piarray[i] = i;
            }
            putchar('\n');
    }
    else {
            puts("int array not allocated");
            exit(0);
    }

    /* allocate a 10 element double array. It
       will not contain predictable values. */

    pdarray = (double *) malloc(10*sizeof(double));

    if (pdarray != NULL) {
            puts("\ndouble array allocated\n");
```

```
                puts("Initial contents are:\n");
                for (i = 0; i < 10; i++)
                        printf("%8.3e\n",pdarray[i]);
        }
        else {
                puts("double array not allocated");
                exit(0);
        }

        /* attempt to allocate a large float array. */

        pfarray = (float *) calloc(30000,sizeof(float));

        if (pfarray != NULL)
                puts("\nfloat array allocated\n");
        else
                puts("float array not allocated");

        /* enlarge int array to 100 elements */

        picopy = piarray; /* save old address */

        piarray = (int *) realloc((char *) piarray,
                        100*sizeof(int));

        if (piarray != NULL) {
                puts("int array enlarged\n");
                if (piarray != picopy)
                        puts("int array moved\n");

                puts("First 12 elements contain:\n");
                for (i = 0; i < 12; i++)
                        printf("%2d ",piarray[i]);
                putchar('\n');
        }
        else
                puts("failed to enlarge int array\n");

        /* release space taken by double array */

        free((char *) pdarray);
}


int array allocated
```

Initial contents are:

0 0 0 0 0 0 0 0 0 0

double array allocated

Initial contents are:

-1.537e-309
-4.393e+290
-8.361e-259
-9.927e+305
4.863e-306
-1.371e-269
-7.273e+197
1.073e+287
1.078e-285
-1.598e-308

float array allocated

int array enlarged

int array moved

First 12 elements contain:

0 1 2 3 4 5 6 7 8 9 -20464 -29942

Conclusion

Much of the information contained in this chapter may never be needed by most C programmers, however, it won't hurt to know it. If you are interfacing with assembler or other languages, generating ROMable code, working with fixed-memory operating systems or with potentially large amounts of temporary data, or you need to allocate a large amount of memory at run-time, you will need to deal with at least some of the concepts mentioned here.

There is no absolute formula for calculating the exact temporary data space requirements for a C program but a reasonable guesstimate will need to be made. One thing to keep in mind is that even though you might come up with such an estimate it may not work for the next version of the same compiler or with other compilers, even on the same machine. Also on systems such as the Intel 8086/88, there are a number of different memory models to chose from, and stack requirements for a given piece of code may depend on the particular model being used.

And just to confuse the issue even further, consider portability. Even if a reasonable estimate of stack size requirements is available, that does not guarantee a program will run on another machine/compiler combination. This kind of problem will likely manifest itself if you are porting C code from a 32-bit machine to one of smaller word size or from a larger Intel model to a smaller one. Again, there is no general solution to this problem.

The X3J11 Draft

A number of things in the proposed draft Standard may affect stack usage. They are:

- A new data type is allowed; `long double`. This may require more storage in memory and on the stack than a `double`.

- Function prototypes have been introduced. This notion permits variables of any type (except arrays) to be passed as arguments without argument widening taking affect. For example, it is possible to pass a `char` or `float` and have only that size variable passed on the stack without it being widened to an `int` or `double`.

- Structures and unions can now be passed by value. The larger the structure (or union), the larger the stack requirements for that argument.

- Enumerations are now supported and enumeration constants may be stored in an `int` or some shorter signed integral type. In the absence of a function prototype, such values are widened to `int` when used as arguments. If a prototype is in force, it dictates the type of the argument to be used.

CHAPTER 5

Headers and the Preprocessor

Any nontrivial C program uses at least one header (usually stdio.h). Headers play an important part in the successful design and implementation of C programs, so much so that this entire chapter is devoted to them. Headers are generally thought of as necessary to access the definition of system library function types and macros. However, they can provide much more capability than this if designed and used correctly. Not only can headers make coding simpler, they can reduce source code size and complexity, they can significantly aid in program documentation and quality assurance, and they are mandatory when writing code that is to be ported across different hardware and/or system software environments.

The Mechanics

A header is an object that can be referenced by a preprocessor #include directive. Note that headers are not referred to as files. That is because, technically, a header need not exist as a separate disk file. While user-defined headers usually do exist in this form, an implementation is at liberty to implement headers in any way it sees fit. The only requirement is that they make the required standard headers available for processing via the #include directive and that application programmers have a mechanism for defining their own headers. Headers, particular system headers, could be defined internal to the compiler, or they might exist in external libraries or as binary rather than text files.

For the purpose of discussion in this chapter, headers will be deemed to reside as character files on disk.

Header Contents

Just what can and should headers contain? There is no restriction on the content of headers provided they contain complete elements. An element is a complete preprocessor directive, language declaration, definition, or statement. Partial elements within a header will be flagged as errors by the compiler. In particular, it is illegal to have an incomplete last element in a header such that the header end-of-file is reached before the element is deemed to be syntactically complete.

To eliminate this possibility, a header must be terminated with a '\n', and any open comment must be closed with a */ token before the end of the header. Likewise, any trailing preprocessor directive must be completed. The last line of a header cannot end with a '\' (which indicates a preprocessor continuation line follows). The last element should not be a partial union or structure declaration or partial language statement.

Most header files contain some combination of #define macros, union, structure, and enum declarations, and typedef and function return type declarations.

There is (generally) little or no value in placing variable definitions in headers because an object can only be defined in one place while the purpose of a header is (generally) to allow its information to be shared by multiple modules. (Note the distinction between a definition and a declaration. A *definition* is a defining instance that results in storage space being allocated, while a *declaration* is a reference to the defining instance.)

Putting executable code (except within simple macro definitions such as max, abs, islower, etc.) in headers also seems to be of little value. Again, the purpose of placing something in a header is so that it can be shared. So the obvious alternative to having a large block of code in a header is to make that code a function. The cost of this is the overhead of the function call, but the approach is more natural. In particular, having a section of code in a header makes the including source file harder to understand without an expanded listing of the header.

Likewise, placing the leading part of or a complete function definition (including its entry point) in a header only obscures the meaning of the including file. Many source file cross-reference utilities do not expand header files. So it would be possible to have a local object referenced several times in the file without having a definition, because the definition exists in a partial code segment in a header.

Justifying a Header

Perhaps the most common use of headers is to group often-used macro definitions and union and structure declarations. Not only does the grouping of these in a common place make logical sense, it can significantly reduce debugging errors due to inconsistent definition and references.

Another common use is in declaring the return value types of library and user-written functions. Omitting the declaration for a function that returns a non-int value will generally result in an error that is not always obvious (except to lint and good interpreters).

```
sub(a)
double a;
{
    double d;

    d = sqrt(a);

}
```

Here, the library function sqrt actually returns a double but this is incorrectly interpreted as an int that is then cast to a double and stored in d, resulting in d being quite wrong. A declaration of the type double sqrt(); should be included. The best way to correct this problem is to use #include <math.h>, which ensures that the return value type of sqrt is correctly declared.

```
f()
{
    char *cptr;
    extern char dest[];

    cptr = strcpy(dest,"string");

}
```

The library function `strcpy` returns a value of type (`char *`), however, this value is interpreted as an `int` and cast to a pointer to `char` before being stored in `cptr`. The unfortunate thing about this error is that the function will work perfectly well on a large number of systems because the size of an `int` and a `char` pointer are identical. It is only when this function is ported to a dissimilar environment that it fails. Fortunately, `lint` and interpreters can detect such a mismatch.

Naming Conventions

Headers have traditionally had names of the format xxx.h, where xxx represents the header name and .h represents the header type. Many modern operating systems support filenames of the same format so the notion of a header actually being a file works well in these environments. These systems typically support filenames of at least 6 alphanumeric characters and so the commonly used system headers (`stdio`, `string`, `assert`, `limits`, etc.) can be named accordingly on disk. Note that system header names contain only alphabetic characters. While file systems may be case sensitive regarding the names of files, the names of the standard headers are always written in lower case.

The header type .h is purely conventional and is redundant in that any object referenced in an `#include` directive is, by definition, a header file. Perhaps the only value of having a header type at all is so that the user can distinguish header files from others when using the operating system's directory listing utility. Also, by establishing this convention, it aids in programmer portability on systems that support header types. If you must put language definitions or executable code in a header you may want to use header types other than .h so these can easily be differentiated at both the file system level and by looking at source code listings.

User-written headers implemented as files can have any name (and type) that is acceptable to their run-time environment. Some operating systems (most noticeably UNIX, VAX/VMS and MS-DOS) have a hierarchical file system that begins with a root directory. This root can have many branches, each of which can also have branches, etc. Programs that execute on such a system (including compilers and interpreters) do so in the context of a run-time environment, one of whose properties is a default home directory. In the absence of a directory specifier, a reference to a filename causes the file system to search the program's default directory.

Such systems also support the notion of a directory search path that specifies the locations and ordering of directory searches if the desired file does not exist in the default place. This path mechanism can be quite useful but it can also be a burden.

Consider the case in which three separate applications each use a different set of header files that are located in directories A, B, and C, respectively. The `#include` directives in each application's programs do not contain any directory location information, only the header file name. Therefore, when these programs are compiled, the path mechanism will be used to locate the headers. Since the path can only be organized in one way (such as first C then A and finally B), it will take longer to locate the headers for some programs than it will for others. If fifteen different programs each have a different header directory, the path definition can become quite cumbersome and slow to traverse. Of course, all of the headers could be grouped in the same (or only a few) directories, but this makes maintenance messier.

One alternative is to hard-code the header directory right into the `#include` directive. However, while this solves the directory search problem, it requires all such source code references to be changed if the header location changes. This is inconvenient particularly when porting programs to another environment where it is impossible or undesirable to use the same header locations. The X3J11 draft allows preprocessor token pasting and this may help solve the problem. See more on this below.

UNIX, MS-DOS and VAX/VMS also allow relative directory references such that given some current default environment, it is possible to reference a file in the next higher or lower level of the file system hierarchy.

Another possible solution to the header location problem is often implemented via an argument on the compiler command-line. This compile-time option might be of the form −ia,b,c, where −i is a switch indicating `#include` file search path and a, b, and c give the locations and ordering of the search if no directory information is included in an `#include` directive. Path capability is not required for this approach, it can be implemented on systems with and without one. It also allows the source code to be oblivious to the actual location of its headers. There will probably be a reasonable limit on the number and/or length of alternate search paths allowed but if the header system is designed properly, no more than three or four header locations should ever be needed for any one project. Of course, this method will cause problems during porting to a compiler that doesn't implement an equivalent include-file switch or that allows fewer alternate paths than are required.

The Preprocessor Symbol Table

As #define macros are encountered in source files and/or headers, their names and definitions are stored in a symbol table. This allows subsequent references to them to be replaced by their corresponding definitions. It also allows the existence and value of macros to be tested using the #ifxxx directives. Macros and headers are handled by the preprocessor, which does *not* have any knowledge about the C language. In its crudest form, the preprocessor is a string substitution utility that uses the symbol table to handle text replacement and conditional directives.

It is important to realize just what objects are stored in this symbol table so that entries can be located and tested in headers and source code modules. The table does not contain any C language object name (like global and auto variables, function names, and labels) or type information. Also, in a program that has three separately compiled source modules, the symbol table starts out empty for each of the three separate compilations. No symbol table information is available between compilations. It is, however, available across multiple functions within the same source code file. (Actually, the table may not be quite empty due to the presence of predefined symbols, as discussed below.)

The relevance of this is that the #ifxxx directives can't be used to check on the existence or value of macros in other source files or headers unless they are #included. Also, the presence or compile-time value of any language object, such as a variable or function, cannot be determined. The preprocessor can only locate and test symbols that were defined within the current source file's scope.

Header Size

When headers are implemented as files, the programmer has direct control over their size. At one extreme, all the header information for an application could be contained in one big header file, and at the other extreme, each header element could have its own header file. Both of these approaches are generally unworkable. The larger a header file the longer the compilation time. With a large number of small headers, a number of them may need to be referenced in each source code module, in which case, directory search time may be significant each time they are opened. Many file systems allocate files in aggregates or clusters, which may be as much as 2K to 8K bytes in which case the disk space cost of having four 100 byte headers versus one 400 byte header, for example, is significant.

The main criteria in deciding just what to put in a particular header has to do with the logical relationships between the elements. Unless a header is specifically classed as miscellaneous and contains elements that don't fit elsewhere, it should only contain closely related elements and it should be named accordingly. In this way, only those headers needed by a module have to be included. If a module does not reference any or most of a large header, the preprocessor will still set up the whole symbol table and test conditionals, etc., even though these will not be used. Actually, for reasonably small source modules it may take longer to preprocess the headers than it does to actually compile the source. Of course, one should keep compile-time importance in perspective, as it has far less ultimate significance than does execution time.

The contents and size of headers should be decided upon before they are first used. Changing the organization of an existing set of headers may take some work and can even introduce new bugs. Header layout and size is an integral part of program design. The size of the compiler's symbol table, in terms of number of entries and total string length, may also be a factor in designing headers, as there is no point designing something that the preprocessor can't handle.

Nesting Headers

Header files can be nested up to some implementation-defined depth. This allows a group of headers to be included using one master include file. For example, if `"system.h"` contains

```
#include <stdio.h>
#include <math.h>
   . . .
#include <string.h>
#include <assert.h>
```

then using `#include "system.h"` causes all of the compiler supplied headers to be included. For most source modules, it is unlikely that more than two or three of these headers will actually be needed, so the desirability of this approach gets back to the compile-time and logical breakdown versus having to specify two or three `#include` directives instead of just one. Unless the set of `#include` files grouped in this way is very closely related, this method probably creates more problems than it solves.

A disadvantage of grouped headers arises when using a search program (such as the UNIX grep utility) to scan a set of source modules to see which ones use a particular header. If header X is part of a group header G then only G can be searched for, not X, and when a match is found, it is not certain if that module actually uses any of header X even though it is indirectly included. This problem also occurs when using make—like tools that automatically recompile any modules that reference a given header file. With grouped headers, these tools could possibly recompile large amounts of code unnecessarily if the included headers are not actually used.

Nested #include files give rise to the possibility of the same header being included more than once for a source module, as follows. A user source module contains

```
#include <stdio.h>
#include "keypad.h"
#include "nodes.h"
```

and keypad.h and nodes.h also both contain #include <stdio.h> so that the header stdio.h is actually referenced three times. One obvious solution might be to remove the references from keypad.h and nodes.h. But what if the user references these headers without referencing stdio.h first? Should the onus be on the programmer to remember which headers require which other headers, or can this all be made transparent? It can be transparent if the headers are properly designed to be totally self-contained.

The main problem with this approach is that headers can define storage space for objects and it is undesirable to have this storage allocated more than once in a module. (Multiple definitions of the same external are definitely not wanted, but there is no way to check for this when the same header is included during different compilations.) Consider the previous example again.

```
#include <stdio.h>
#include "keypad.h"
#include "nodes.h"
```

If the following directives are added to stdio.h

```
#ifndef STDIO_H
#define STDIO_H
    . . .
stdio.h definitions and declarations
    . . .
#endif
```

---

it would never be included more than once in any one compilation. Likewise, user-defined headers such as keypad.h can be arranged like

---

```
#ifndef KEYPAD_H
#define KEYPAD_H
    . . .
keypad.h definitions and declarations
    . . .
#endif
```

Each header has a corresponding macro of the same name, written in upper case. This approach requires that you reserve these names ahead of time so they don't conflict with other macros, and it is important that you use a systematic naming convention for these header ID macros to aid in programmer portability.

This method requires system headers such as stdio.h to be modified, not a very desirable task since these headers will get superseded when a new version of the compiler is installed, and unless you remember to put the changes in the new versions, the problem will reappear. (Actually the standard header files provided by most vendors do not contain object definitions, so there is no problem in their being included multiple times other than the extra time taken to reprocess them.)

System and Standard Headers

System and standard headers have been mentioned in several places above. A standard header is one that is generally found in C environments and has very similar contents (or at least a similar purpose) in each of those environments. Examples of standard headers are stdio.h, math.h, ctype.h, and setjmp.h. System headers are those provided with a compiler that give access to some particular aspect of the compiler's hardware or software environment, such as operating system and file system characteristics.

Location and Access

System and standard headers have usefulness beyond any particular application and should therefore be placed in a universally accessible place so that one central copy can be shared by all programs. This also means that any changes or updates to these headers need only be done in that one place making the system maintenance task easier. If these headers must reside in multiple places, there needs to be a mechanism to ensure that all versions are correctly updated.

System and standard headers should be considered sacred in that they should not be changed without first giving significant thought to the impact of such changes. Therefore, it is highly recommended that they reside in a directory such that programmers can only get read access to them. Only system managers should be able to modify these headers since they provide a significant key to program integrity. Even if one project group can justify certain additions or changes, the impact on other projects must be considered.

Single-user operating systems often do not have any file access protection so header integrity is at the mercy of the programmer. Such systems may not support a hierarchical or multiple directory structure, in which case system, standard, and application headers may all exist in the same directory. In this case, the <...> and "..." conventions should still be used with the #include directive to provide information about the origins of these headers.

Predefined Symbols

It is common practice for compilers to have knowledge of some predefined macros. These macros need not be the subject of a #define directive by the user, as their names and values (if any) are built into the compiler. A list of these macros is normally provided in the vendor documentation. These macros often contain information about the type of hardware, operating system, and run-time environment. For example:

Macro	Meaning
VAX11	DEC VAX—11 series CPU
PDP11	DEC PDP—11
I8086	Intel 8086/8088
M68000	Motorola 680x0
UNIX	UNIX operating system
PCDOS	IBM's PC—DOS
MSDOS	Microsoft's MS—DOS
RSX11M	DEC's RSX—11M series
CPM80	DRI's CP/M—80
VAXVMS	DEC's VAX/VMS

Some machines support multiple hardware modes. For instance, the Intel 8086/8088 allows various memory models that each have different combinations of code and data sizes. Usually, compilers on such systems support a command-line switch to allow users to specify which model they want to use, in which case the corresponding macro becomes predefined. For example:

Macro	Meaning
I8086S	Intel small memory model
I8086L	Intel large memory model

There is no universal naming convention for these predefined macros, so it is possible that PDP and PDP11 will both refer to a DEC PDP-11 series processor.

Approaches to `ctype.h`

The header `ctype.h` declares several mechanisms useful for testing and mapping characters. These include

---

```
int isalnum(int c)
int isalpha(int c)
int isdigit(int c)
int islower(int c)
int isupper(int c)
int tolower(int c)
int toupper(int c)
```

These mechanisms are implemented in one of two ways: as real functions or as macros. The function approach is quite straightforward. It simply requires that each routine be written and placed in the run-time library. In this case, `ctype.h` will just contain the return type declaration for each of these functions (they are, in fact, the default type, `int`).

The macro form can also be implemented in two ways: one as straight in-line macro expansions that are totally self-contained, or by using some predefined lookup table (often called `_ctype_` or something similar). The former approach uses something like

---

```
#define islower(c) ((c) >= 'a' && (c) <= 'z')
```

---

while the latter uses

```
#define islower(c) (_ctype_[(c)+1]) & _LOWER
```

The latter approach is much faster, because it uses a table lookup rather than a block of test code. The table _ctype_ is a predefined list indexed by character set internal values such that for the ASCII character set, the expression _ctype_[65 + 1] contains status information about the character 'A'. This table is defined in the startup module, which is linked in with a user program, and each of its elements contains flags that indicate such things as whether the corresponding character is upper or lower case, if it is a decimal (or hexadecimal) digit, or if it is a space or a punctuation character. By using this static table and a set of macros such as _LOWER (the lower case flag), the various character comparisons and conversions can be done simply with a logical AND or OR as shown in the definition of the islower macro above.

Third-Party Application Libraries

There is an increasing number of applications libraries being sold by independent software developers particularly for microcomputer compilers. These libraries include support for file and record access methods, graphics and windowing, data entry and packed decimal arithmetic, and many include a set of headers.

While library headers can be thought of as application program headers, they can have a life beyond a specific application and so they should reside in the same directory as system and standard headers and be protected accordingly. If you chose to locate them in a directory other than that used by standard and applications headers, there is no way to easily identify such headers via the <...> and "..." #include conventions, as these are the only two such methods of designating locations. In this case, library headers would be treated as system headers and located via a search path mechanism provided at the compiler or operating system level.

When designing an application's header structure, it is useful to know exactly which library headers will be used, so that naming conventions can be integrated. In the event that library headers may contain definitions, the earlier discussion on multiple header inclusion should be kept in mind.

Future versions of the library may contain new headers (and possibly even changes to existing ones), so upgrading may require some planning and possible code changes, particularly if there are naming conflicts with the new header file names and/or library macro names. Similar problems may also occur when using a library with different compilers (although many libraries are available in a number of compiler-specific versions).

Application Headers

Any header not supplied with a compiler or library package or not intended for use as a system or standard header is an application header. This means that the scope of an application header is the particular application for which it was designed.

Location and Access

Application headers should not be in a universally accessible place. They should, however, be available to all developers involved with their particular project. Like system headers, access to applications headers by programmers should normally be limited to read-only mode. Only project managers should be able to modify them, as they provide a significant key to program integrity.

Some systems (typically those that support only one user) do not have file protection or multiple directories, so all headers may exist in the same directory. In this case, the $<...>$ and "$...$" conventions should still be used with the #include directive to provide information about the origins of these headers.

The "$...$" method of referencing headers results in some current or default directory path being searched. On multiperson projects, it is common for each developer to have his or her own testing environment. While headers can be developed and tested within any one of these environments, final versions of them should be moved to a separate (and protected) application header area where they can be shared. It is very undesirable to have multiple production versions of headers. Since it is possible for finished headers to exist in multiple directories, all such locations must be listed on any search path list and that path list must be defined for each developer on that project. Hard-coding of header locations requires code changes if that location changes, whereas the path approach requires only the path to be redefined.

Function Return Types

One primary use for headers is to define the return types of library and user-written functions. In Justifying a Header, above, the problems that can occur with function type mismatches were discussed. To make such header files complete, it is a good idea to also explicitly declare functions that return an int (the default type) value.

A more recent addition to the C language is the void function type. Functions that do not return a value are often defined (and declared) to return the default type int. This is inconsistent and the notion of a void type has been introduced to correct this deficiency.

```
f( )
{
      extern g( );
      int i;

      i = g( );
}
g( )
{
      return;
}
```

Here, function g is expected to return an int that is subsequently stored in i. Since g does not return a value, yet the default return type of g is int, an int of unknown value will be returned and placed in i. By using void this problem can be eliminated, as follows:

```
f( )
{
      extern void g( );
      int i;

      i = g( );
}

void g( )
{
      return;
}
```

Function g is explicitly declared and defined to be of type void so the statement i = g(); should generate a compilation error because the program attempts to use the return value of a function that does not have one. Likewise, an attempt to return a value from a function that has type void, should also generate an error (e.g., if return (5); were used in function g).

The void type is relatively new and many compilation environments do not yet support it directly, so while the above approach can be implemented using a typedef, as shown below, any discrepancies that exist cannot be detected and reported. The only advantage in this case is that using void where it genuinely exists helps document the code and ultimately makes for an easier transition to support for void when it becomes available.

```
typedef int void;
```

In this case, void is merely a synonym for int, so it doesn't actually work as if void were fully supported as a function type.

Defining Custom Types

It is common practice for programmers to define their own data types using #define or, more likely, typedef. These pseudotypes (or simply types) can have more meaningful names and they allow otherwise complicated object references to be given simple synonyms. They can also greatly assist in writing portable code by isolating the host environment characteristics from the program (and into one or a small number of headers). Examples of such types are

---

```
#define GLOBAL extern
#define FAST register int
typedef struct {double real, imag;} COMPLEX;
typedef unsigned char BYTE;
typedef struct _iobuf FILE;
```

If an application is moved from one environment to another, it is highly likely that the definition of FILE for the new environment will be different, as file pointers are inherently implementation-defined. By using the pseudotype FILE, only those file pointer references in headers need be located and changed.

There are several types implemented in the standard headers of newer compilers. These include ptrdiff_t (the integral type of the result of subtracting two pointers) and size_t (the integral type of the result of the sizeof operator). If these types are not supported by your compiler (they are required by the proposed X3J11 draft), it is a simple matter to implement them using typedef.

```
#include <stdio.h>

typedef unsigned int size_t;

main()
{
    extern size_t strlen();

    printf("%d ",strlen("qwerty"));
    printf("%d ",strlen(""));
}

size_t strlen(string)
char *string;
{
    size_t length = 0;

    while (*string++ != '\0')
            ++length;

    return (length);
}


6   0
```

This example demonstrates the ability to write portable code. In reality, the definition of size_t and the return type declaration of strlen would be contained in a standard header such as `string.h`, in which case only that header need be changed if `size_t` is not of type `unsigned int`.

Concurrent Development on Different Systems

It is possible that programmers working on the same project are using different (and possibly nonconnected) development systems. (This is particularly true with single-user microcomputers running CP/M or MS-DOS.) In such an environment, multiple copies of headers are needed, one for each development system, and this can lead to discrepancies in header content. Unless a tested master version of each header is propagated to each system on a regular basis, there may be considerable difficulty in merging the individual's efforts. Apart from having mismatched versions, each may have used the same macro names for different purposes, a problem that may not become immediately obvious.

Distributed development environments require even more management and discipline than is needed on multi-user hosts.

The `extern` Define/Reference Problem

In any nontrivial project the need will arise to have some externals defined in one source module and declared in one or more other modules. A common approach to this problem is to define the objects in the main source module and place the external declarations in a header that is included in other source files as necessary. Consider the following excerpt from a text processing program.

```
/* define and initialize globals */

int lm = 1;                 /* left margin */
int rm = 80;                /* right margin */
int cnumber = 0;            /* current chapter # */
int pgwidth = 80;           /* page width in chars */
int pglength = 65;          /* page length in lines */
int pgnumber = 0;           /* current page # */

main(argc,argv)
int argc;
char *argv[];
```

```
{
    ...
}

/*
txtgbl.h - text processor global header file
*/

extern int lm;              /* left margin */
extern int rm;              /* right margin */
extern int cnumber;         /* current chapter # */
extern int pgwidth;         /* page width in chars */
extern int pglength;        /* page length in lines */
extern int pgnumber;        /* current page # */
```

The global objects are defined and initialized in the main source module and they are declared in a header called `txtgbl.h`.

```
#include "txtgbl.h"

sub()
{
    ...
}
```

Function `sub` references these globals properly by including the header `txtgbl.h`.

This approach is often used, but if a new global is added or an existing one is changed, both the main routine and the header need to be modified, as the definitions and declarations are kept in separate files. The following example shows a slightly different solution.

```
#define MAIN
#include "txtgbl.h"
#undef MAIN

main(argc,argv)
int argc;
char *argv[];
{
...
}

/*
txtgbl.h - revised version
*/

#ifdef MAIN

int lm = 1;                /* left margin */
int rm = 80;               /* right margin */
int cnumber = 0;           /* current chapter # */
int pgwidth = 80;          /* page width in chars */
int pglength = 65;         /* page length in lines */
int pgnumber = 0;          /* current page # */

#else

extern int lm;             /* left margin */
extern int rm;             /* right margin */
extern int cnumber;        /* current chapter # */
extern int pgwidth;        /* page width in chars */
extern int pglength;       /* page length in lines */
extern int pgnumber;       /* current page # */

#endif
```

Here, the main source file contains no global definitions. The definitions and the declarations both reside in the header file `txtgbl.h` and are selected based on whether or not the macro MAIN is currently defined. When the `main` file is compiled, the object definitions are included, whereas when other files (such as that containing function `sub`) are compiled, the object declarations are included. The function `sub` remains the same as in the earlier example.

While this method requires the introduction of the macro MAIN, it does allow both the definitions and declarations to reside in the same header and that makes it easier to modify or add to the object list. With these in the same header, there is less likelihood that definitions and declarations will get out of step when changes to them are made.

A more exotic (and restricted) version of this header is as follows.

```
/*
txtgbl.h - exotic, limited version
*/

#ifdef MAIN
#define CLASS
#else
#define CLASS extern
#endif

CLASS int lm;               /* left margin */
CLASS int rm;               /* right margin */
CLASS int cnumber;          /* current chapter # */
CLASS int pgwidth;          /* page width in chars */
CLASS int pglength;         /* page length in lines */
CLASS int pgnumber;         /* current page # */

#undef CLASS
```

The value of this approach is that there really is only one place for both the definition and declaration. The problem is that the definitions cannot contain initializers and this is a significant limitation as it is not usually desirable to have all globals default to a value of zero. (Note that some compilers do allow initializers on both definitions and declarations.)

The following example shows how to achieve both declaration and initialization in the same header.

```
/*
txtgbl.h — exotic and complete version
*/

#ifdef MAIN
#define CLASS
#else
#define CLASS extern
#endif

CLASS int lm            /* left margin */
#ifdef MAIN
 = 1
#endif
;

CLASS int rm            /* right margin */
#ifdef MAIN
 = 80
#endif
;

CLASS int cnumber       /* current chapter # */
#ifdef MAIN
 = 0
#endif
;

CLASS int pgwidth       /* page width in chars */
#ifdef MAIN
 = 80
#endif
;

CLASS int pglength      /* page length in lines */
#ifdef MAIN
 = 65
#endif
;
```

```
CLASS int pgnumber        /* current page # */
#ifdef MAIN
  = 0
#endif
;

#undef CLASS
```

To many programmers, this solution may appear to be worse than the problem and that may be the case. However, it is presented as another possible alternative.

Our discussion thus far has been limited to the simple case in which all globals are defined in the same source module but this may not be the case. Globals can be defined in any source module and referenced in any other module. If such definitions are spread throughout many modules, it can be quite difficult to come up with a logical approach to header design that allows no multiple definition conflicts.

There seems to be no reason to have these definitions spread throughout the modules other than that is where the programmer decided they were needed so that's where they were defined. With a large, multiprogrammer project it is very important to define the complete global object data dictionary before significant amounts of code are written. Then all (or the vast majority) of these definitions can be grouped into the same source module, preferably the one containing function `main`. This means that all programmers know exactly where to find global definitions, and if this list is kept in alphabetical order by name within data type, it can serve as the project's on-line data dictionary. Also any explicit initializers could be easily identified.

Removing Macro Definitions

The #undef preprocessor directive is used to remove the definition of the object from a previous #define. While #undef is not often used, it can be quite useful in a number of circumstances. If too many macros are defined or the total string length of all defined macros exceeds the table size of the compiler then some of them must be undefined before the remainder can be added. If you plan on having large numbers of macros and/or large macro definitions, you will need to plan for this possibility.

Some compilation environments implement library capabilities as both macros and functions (e.g. `islower`, `isalpha`, `tolower`, etc.). It is possible

161

that macro expansions of these routines may have undesirable side affects or create too much in-line code, in which case the function version might be preferred. In such implementations, the function name is hidden by a macro definition of the same name (either in a standard header such as stdio.h or as a predefined macro), so to gain access to the function, the #undef directive must be used.

Some systems allow nonexistent macros to be #undef-ed, while others don't. Likewise, some systems assume the value of a nonexistent macro to be zero when used with #if, while others will generate an error.

It is probably unwise to place #undef directives inside a header, because their presence would not be obvious, and as the use of #undef has significant meaning, occurrences of it should stand out (and should be accompanied by a comment explaining the reason).

Placement and Ordering of Directives

#include directives should appear at the beginning of a header or source module with the system/standard headers listed first, followed by library headers, then application headers. Any #define and #undef directives that have no bearing on subsequent header includes should be specified after all includes as follows.

```
#include <stdio.h>
#undef tolower

#define TEST
#include "table.h"

#define EOS '\0'
#define CR '\r'
```

By grouping preprocessor directives and separating groups with a blank line, some meaning can be implied. For example, the definition of the macro tolower is removed immediately after stdio.h is included. So it can be assumed that it was defined in that header, and as TEST is defined immediately before table.h is included, one might assume that it somehow affects the way in which this header is processed. Finally, the macros EOS and CR come after all the other directives, so it can be assumed they are purely local definitions. This grouping can provide significant information for very little effort and it can greatly assist program maintenance and programmer portability.

There is no point in including headers that are not used. This will only serve to confuse you when you use module search tools to locate header references and when using make—like tools to rebuild all or part of a system.

Portability Considerations

The sizeof compile-time operator may seem like it would be very useful when writing code to be portable across different machine architectures.

```
#if sizeof(int) == 2
long count;
#else
int count;
#endif
```

This code will work on some systems, but it is outlawed by the proposed X3J11 draft because the preprocessor technically does not know anything about the structure of the C language, including the nature of an int. The sizeof operator is only recognized by the compiler, not the preprocessor.

Not all compilers recognize identifiers containing more than 8 character names. It is possible that you may need to port code from one that does to one that doesn't and in the process you find that the first 8 characters of some names are not unique. Once these names have been identified, they can be given shorter aliases in a header as follows.

```
#define very_long_name alias
#define another_name new_name
```

This allows the existing code to be used without modification once an appropriate header file has been included. It should be considered a temporary fix, as it may be difficult to ensure that the alias names are themselves

163

unique and meaningful. Also, when using a symbolic debugger with such a program, the user must use the alias name, not the long version from the source code.

Other areas to consider when porting are the size of the preprocessor symbol table for both number and total size of entries, the complexity of nested #if directives, and the level of nested #includes.

The X3J11 Draft

A number of points regarding the preprocessor in the proposed ANSI Standard are worth mentioning. They are:

- The standard headers are sacred. They should never be modified or extended by the user and there are strict limits on what an implementer can place in them. This is designed to aid portability by making their contents very predictable. The proposed standard headers and their purposes are defined in Appendix A.

- The NULL macro is now defined as either (void *)0, 0, or 0L. The former is the value zero cast to a pointer to void.

- The types ptrdiff_t (type of difference between two pointers) and size_t (type of sizeof return value) have been introduced. These are discussed earlier in this chapter.

- Identifiers beginning with one underscore are reserved by the language and language implementers while those beginning with two underscores can be used by implementers.

- The macros __LINE__ and __FILE__ are predefined and contain the current source line number (in decimal) and the presumed name of the current source file respectively.

- The predefined macro name __DATE__ has the value of the date of translation of the source file, stored in a string with the format

---

"mmm dd yyyy".

164

- The predefined macro __TIME__ has the value of the time of translation of the source file, stored in a string with the format.

"hh:mm:ss".

- The notion of function prototypes has been added. These allow a function type and argument list template to be declared so that argument list count, ordering, and type checking can be implemented. For example:

```
ctype.h          int toupper(int);
math.h           double sqrt(double);
stdio.h          char *fgets(char *, int, FILE *);
```

When these headers are included, the above prototypes are declared. They declare each function's return type and the order and type of its arguments. There is also annotation for an argument list with a fixed leading part and a trailing variable part as used in the printf and scanf family of routines.

- Conforming programs—Even if a library function returns a default type value of int, the appropriate standard header should be included. If it is not, the program is not a strictly conforming one. For example:

```
main()
{
    printf("Hello world\n");
}
```

---

is not strictly conforming as it does not contain #include <stdio.h>.

- Preprocessor directives may be preceded with any number of spaces and/or horizontal tabs. These same separators may exist between the # and directive identifier such as in `#  include <...>`.

The `#include` directive can also be of the form

```
#include identifier
```

---

where the identifier is a macro name that has a value of the form $<...>$ or `"..."`. This allows code like

---

```
#define HEADER "header.h"
#include HEADER
```

This may not seem to be of much use, but when coupled with the new `##` preprocessor concatenation operator, it allows elaborate header file references to be constructed dynamically. This is known as token pasting and one possible use for it is in handling headers that reside in specific directories and it is undesirable to hard-code these directory names into the `#include` directive. By defining a macro to contain the physical device/directory location, it is possible to prepend this to the header name such that all such header references are relative to the value of the defined macro. In this case, if the header location is changed, only one macro definition need be altered and the source recompiled.

- Several new directives and operators have been added. `#elif` is a shorthand way of implementing multiway `#if`/`#else` tests; `#pragma` is an implementation-defined directive that is ignored by systems that do not recognize it; and the null directive `#`, which is just ignored. A preprocessor-only operator has been added to aid in testing the existence of identifiers. Its form is

---

```
              defined identifier
    or    defined (identifier)
```

This operator allows complex conditional expressions such as

```
#if defined(TEST) && !defined(MAIN)
   . . .
#endif
```

- If the preprocessor fails to locate a header referenced by "...", the #include directive is reprocessed as if the < ... > form were used.

- A large number of new library functions, macros and typedefs have been added in the proposed Standard and these are reserved by the language. (Certain other identifiers are also reserved for future use, such as library function names beginning with str and mem.) Even if a particular header is not used by a program, the identifiers defined in that header are reserved and in the interests of portability (or at least Standard conformance) the identifiers should not be used for other purposes. So rather than just sitting down and inventing identifiers on the spur of the moment, programmers must make sure their identifiers don't conflict with those in standard headers. This alone strengthens the case for constructing a complete identifier data dictionary during the project design phase.

CHAPTER 6

Program Startup and Termination

To most programmers, a C program starts and ends with the function `main`. However, depending on the implementation, a considerable (and very important) amount of work may be done both before and after function `main` (and hence the user program) is run. While a working knowledge of the specific details of this work is not required to write efficient and correct programs for a particular implementation, porting programs from one implementation to another may require that the two systems support similar startup and termination facilities and such facilities do not always exist.

Introduction

All functions in C have exactly the same structure; they have a name and optional argument list, at least one block of executable code (which may be empty), and they may optionally return a value. Function `main` is no exception except, that by using the function name `main`, somehow magically the program will begin execution at that point.

Languages typically have a different structure for a program's main module (compared to that of other subroutines), so that the actual entry point to the executable module can be determined (e.g., FORTRAN uses PROGRAM, Pascal uses `program`, and the main entry point routine in assembly language programs is usually terminated differently than are subroutines). C does not differentiate between modules in this way, it just gives some extra meaning to a function named `main`. Therefore, it must be assumed that either the compiler does something special when compiling `main` or that some run-time envelope surrounds the actual user program and passes control to it via `main`.

The fact that main can have arguments (argc and argv) just like any other C function implies that main can be invoked by another routine, and this is indeed the case. Therefore, main cannot be the actual entry point for the program. The startup code in the run-time envelope does its job and then calls main, passing it the arguments argc and argv. (Note that main can also call itself recursively, and while this isn't particularly useful, it further emphasizes the fact that main is just another function.)

For the purpose of this discussion, the run-time envelope (or environment) will be referred to by the name of _main. (This name is used for that purpose by a number of commercial implementations.) Apart from setting up and passing argc and argv to main just what does _main do? It sets up the stack so that auto variables can be defined and function argument lists can be stored; it reserves space for the heap so that malloc and calloc can dynamically allocate space at run-time; it makes sure that the special files stdin, stdout, and stderr are opened properly; and it ensures that a program terminates gracefully. It may perform numerous other tasks depending on the hardware and system software environment in which it is to run. The more important functions typically performed by _main will be discussed in detail below.

C programs may be run in one of two types of environment: hosted or freestanding. In a hosted implementation, the program is loaded and executed under the control of an operating system or monitor. With this model _main is an integral part of the user program executable module and is indeed the program's physical starting point (whereas main is the logical starting point). In a freestanding environment _main may not exist. Here, the program does not run under a traditional operating system and its startup and termination procedures are entirely programmer-dependent. Such a program need not have either _main nor main present; the program can begin anywhere its implementer desires.

Throughout this chapter, a hosted environment will be implied unless specifically stated otherwise.

The Command-Line Interface

The arguments passed to main by _main are argc and argv. (Others may be passed and these will be discussed later.) These arguments contain information about the command-line used to invoke this particular program. argc is an int and contains the number of arguments found, while argv is an array of pointers to these arguments. The format of a command-line is

```
progname arg1 arg2 ... argn
```

where `progname` is the method used to load and run the program (perhaps by naming it) and `arg1` through `argn` are optional arguments. A command-line argument is deemed to be a non-white-space character string. Consecutive arguments are separated by multiple spaces and/or horizontal tabs. Regardless of the type of character in an argument, arguments are always considered to be character strings (e.g., the integer argument 12345 is interpreted as the string "12345").

Command-line arguments are made available to the program so that it can take corresponding action. The argument list may contain input and/or output filenames that the program should use or it may contain switches that change the way in which the program works, perhaps by overriding certain default values. For example, when a text processing program `textpro` is invoked using

```
textpro infile outfile
```

it uses certain default values such as single spacing, left margin of 5, right margin of 75, and so on, as it reads the input document file `infile` and creates the formatted version in file `outfile`. If the same program were invoked as

```
textpro infile outfile /spacing=2 /lm=1 /rm=80
```

then these default settings would be overridden (provided of course that `textpro` was programmed to recognize and process these switches). The advantage of this approach is that the same raw document file can be formatted quite differently just by running `textpro` with different combinations of command-line arguments. The raw file need not be changed.

The same results could be obtained without using command-line arguments by forcing the program to explicitly prompt the user to enter them, and this is in fact done by some system utilities on the VAX/VMS and RSX operating systems. If they don't detect sufficient (or any) command-line arguments, they prompt for the rest. The problem with this approach is that it requires an interactive dialogue each time the program is run, and unless a batch file of canned answers can be fed to the program in place of this interaction, the program cannot be run unattended. By allowing command-line arguments, these programs can be run in batch mode or can be invoked directly by other tasks. Such methods are common and easy to use on UNIX, MS-DOS, VAX/VMS, and other operating systems.

Command-Line Size

The maximum length of a command-line is set by the operating environment and may vary considerably from one system to another. When designing an application, the number and format of the command-line arguments that will be accepted as valid, needs to be decided. For a text processing program there might literally be hundreds of different switches that could qualify as command-line arguments, however, this would require a very large command-line and would also require the user to type in a lengthy and error-prone argument list.

Obviously, it is not a good idea to design a set of command-line switches such that together they would exceed the maximum command-line buffer size for the system. If a user is used to having a 100-character command-line buffer available for a program and if that program is ported to a system whose maximum buffer size is 80, this may have significant consequences.

Several approaches can be taken to reduce the size requirements of the command-line buffer. The most common value for a command-line switch should be hard-coded into the program as the default value (or read from a profile) such that it only need be specified as an argument if other than that default value is required. A number of command-line processors (including DEC's DCL) allow arguments to be abbreviated. For example, the command-line

```
directory *.* /date /time /size
```

could be abbreviated to

172

```
dire *.* /d /t /s
```

---

provided that the switch abbreviations are not ambiguous. If two switches have the same leading characters, then enough characters must be specified such that the switch abbreviations are no longer exactly the same.

Another possibility is to have a command-line argument that points to a file that contains the program's startup profile. In this way, an infinite number of startup arguments can be defined for the cost of just one command-line argument.

Another aspect of the command-line worth considering is the maximum number of arguments possible because, along with the maximum buffer length, this may affect the porting of an application that can potentially have many (or large) arguments. For a buffer n characters long, the maximum number of arguments is $(n+1)/2$ assuming that each argument can be as small as 1 character and that successive arguments are separated by 1 space (or tab).

The Availability of `argv[0]`

The command-line arguments are available to `main` through `argv[0]`, `argv[1]`, ..., `argv[argc-1]`, where `argc` is the argument count. Arguments are processed left to right with the leftmost argument being pointed to by `argv[0]`. Traditionally, operating systems require that the first command-line argument be used to identify the program is to be run. This means that the program test can be run using something like

---

```
test qqq www eee
```

---

but not like

```
qqq test www eee
```

173

In the latter case, the system's loader will try to locate and load program qqq.

Some systems (most notably releases of MS-DOS prior to version 3.0) do not preserve this first argument. Once the loader has found the program named in the first argument, it passes the remaining command-line characters to the program for further processing. It does *not* pass argv[0]. By definition, a command-line must contain at least one argument, the name of the program (or command) to be run, so whether or not argv[0] is actually passed to _main, argc will always be at least one. On systems where argv[0] is not made available by the operating system, some dummy string such as "", "c", or "prog" is passed.

Few applications need to access argv[0]. All they care about is that they are running regardless of the method used to invoke them. Some command-line processors such as DEC's DCL allow multiple aliases and other methods to be used to reference exactly the same executable module. In such an environment, there may be some benefit to the program in knowing exactly how it was started.

The Case of argv Strings

Most modern operating environments support character sets that contain both upper- and lower-case letters, although command-line processors for some of these may restrict letters to one case. If you plan on porting programs across multiple environments, you may be interested to see what characters are valid on command-lines for each. Not only is case of concern here, but also whether or not the desired character is allowed (or exists). For example, certain characters in the EBCDIC character set do not exist in ASCII. Therefore, it is suggested that you rely only on the mainstream printable characters for command-line arguments.

Redirection, Pipes, and Filters

One significant part of the philosophy of UNIX is that of filter programs (or simply filters). The idea of a filter is that it performs some fairly straight-forward operation and usually involves no more than one input and output file. Filters often read their input from the standard input device (i.e., the keyboard) and write to the standard output device (i.e., a screen or printer) and they have no notion of devices and hence contain no file manipulation.

If the standard input and/or output can be redirected at the command-line interface level, that filter can be used to read and write from any device and/or file supported by the operating system. The MS-DOS `sort` filter is a good example.

```
sort <indata >outdata /+5
```

`Sort` is a simple string sort program. It sorts records read from standard input according to default values and/or command-line switches (such as /+5) and writes the sorted output to standard output. The redirection characters < and > are used by UNIX and MS-DOS (and other systems) to represent an overriding input and output file/device respectively. Therefore, in this example, sort will read from `indata` and write to `outdata`. The `sort` filter is oblivious to the actual file/device that it is reading from and writing to as the necessary device characteristics are handled at the command-line level. `Sort` can be much simpler than if it had to contend with all possible device and file types; it can just concentrate on its primary task, that of sorting.

Another common redirection specifier is >>, which signifies that the file specified should be opened in append mode whereas > causes an existing file by the same name to be overwritten.

Consider the case in MS-DOS of getting a sorted directory listing. This can be done by

---

```
dir >dir.lst
sort <dir.lst >srtdir.lst /+1
del dir.lst
```

---

but this requires the creation (and explicit deletion of the temporary file `dir.lst`. The need to solve this problem leads to the idea of piping in which the standard output of one program can be piped in as the standard input of another program as follows.

```
dir | sort >srtdir.lst /+1
```

175

The | character is traditionally used as the pipe symbol. There is no limit on the number of programs that can be connected using the pipe mechanism beyond the maximum size of the command-line buffer. By using redirection and piping, it is possible to design a set of simple, single-purpose filters that, when connected via pipes, can perform quite powerful sequences of operations.

Many operating systems do not support redirection and pipes as described above in which case these characters are treated just like any other command-line character and are passed to _main intact. In this case, _main could implement all or some of these capabilities itself. This possibility is explored later in this chapter. On systems that do support these special command-line operators, these characters and their adjacent strings are removed from the command-line before it is passed to _main. They are also omitted from the argc count passed to main.

The _main **Routine**

As mentioned earlier _main can have a number of varied tasks to perform before it passes control to the user function main. Oftentimes _main is made up of two routines, one written in assembler, the other in C. Since some of the tasks of _main may involve the setting of hardware registers (for the stack and heap) and the detection of certain hardware characteristics, they must be done at the assembly code level. Other tasks, such as the setting up of argc and argv, can be done at a higher level and as such might well be written in C. For simplicity, the actual way in which _main is implemented will be ignored and only its common functions will be discussed.

Definition of Arguments to main

When _main is invoked, it is passed the address of a command-line buffer (provided this capability is supported), which may or may not include the first argument as described above as argv[0]. _main then parses this buffer, looking for the start of each string argument, and consequently sets up the arguments argc and argv that it eventually passes to main.

One common way in which the argv array is set up is that space for it (and argc) is allocated in _main and then the command-line buffer is parsed with the address of each argument being stored in successive entries in argv. At the same time, a terminating '\0' is added to each argument found in the command-line buffer overwriting the space or tab previously at that location. (If there is no trailing white-space on the command-line then this method requires that there be room at the end of the command-line buffer to accommodate the trailing '\0' for the last argument.) If the command-line buffer resides in an area that cannot be written to by ˍmain then the buffer must be copied to a place within ˍmain before it can be modified.

If argc and argv are set up by a C function, they could be defined in four possible ways: as globals, static externals, auto variables, or internal statics. All four methods work, although if globals are used they might be accidentally modified by other functions within the program. Since the life of ˍmain begins before main and exists beyond that of main, these arguments can reliably be defined as auto. ˍmain typically invokes main using something like

```
#define MXCMDARG 32

_main(cmdline)
char *cmdline;
{
    int argc;
    char *argv[MXCMDARG];

    . . .

    main(argc, argv);
    . . .

}
```

In this case, argc and argv are passed as arguments to main using the implementation argument passing conventions (possibly via the stack). Both arguments are passed by value, however, as argv is an array of pointers, main could in theory modify the contents of any command-line string, so it is important to know if argv is stored in a writable area if this capability is necessary.

The size of argv in ˍmain is usually fixed when it is compiled, limiting the number of command-line arguments (although not their lengths) that it can hold, so the maximum number of entries might be of interest when designing a command-line argument structure for an application. If the source code to ˍmain is available, this number could be altered as necessary.

One of the tasks often performed by _main is the setting up of an area of memory called the heap, which is used by the run-time library memory management routines (e.g., malloc and calloc) to allocate and deallocate memory dynamically at run-time. If this task is performed before argv is set up, then argv could be created on the heap such that it only uses as much space as it needs and also has no size limit (except that of the heap). Note that the size of the heap need not be fixed during program startup.

Considering the text processing program again, it may be desirable to have a command-line switch that allows an overriding page title or subtitle to be specified such as

```
textpro ... /title="The C Language"
```

The problem here is how to handle arguments with embedded spaces (or possibly tabs) as these characters typically signal the division between adjacent arguments. Ideally the title argument is to be passed to main such that

```
argv[n] points to /title="The C Language"
```

If, however, the quotes surrounding the literal are not specially handled, main might receive the following three arguments instead.

```
argv[n]   - /title="The
argv[n+1] - C
argv[n+2] - Language"
```

The detection and subsequent processing (if any) of such switches is usually the job of _main, so it can use whatever method it likes. It may chose to use single quotes or some character other than '"' to delimit such strings, or it may do nothing and pass them through to `main`. Both approaches are common, so as white-space within arguments may not always be handled exactly as you want, you may wish to design your switch system without it. An alternate and common word connector is the underscore as used in

```
textpro ... /left_margin=5 /page_length=30
```

However, this approach can be messy when using switches like /title, above because all underscores within quoted strings must eventually be replaced by spaces before being used. And what happens if an underscore is really required?

Another, equally messy, approach is to to call a routine as soon as `main` is entered, passing it `argc` and `argv`. If it detects any leading quotes on arguments (passed straight through by _main), it can concatenate subsequent `argv` elements until a closing quote is found. Of course it must adjust `argc` and `argv` accordingly. This method guarantees that regardless of whether or not _main handles embedded white-space correctly the user's program will always get arguments in a predefined way. There are a couple of limitations to this approach. First, if an argument contains multiple and consecutive white-space characters, these will be reduced to just one space. For example,

```
prog /title="The World  -  A Geography"
```

will be returned as

```
prog /title="The World - A Geography"
```

where the two spaces on each side of the hyphen are reduced to one space.

The second problem is that `argv` must be writable and there must be sufficient space at the end of a string pointed to by `argv[n]` such that subsequent `argv` strings can be appended. It is not always possible to guarantee the latter, so it may be best to allocate some new space using `malloc` and store the reconstructed argument there and point the corresponding `argv` entry to that new location.

On systems where command-line processing is supported, the arguments `argc` and `argv` are always passed to `main` even if `argc` only equals one. The programmer is quite at liberty to define `main` without any arguments, in which case any passed to it by `_main` are ignored. However, if `main` does declare arguments, it usually has two (`argc` and `argv`) on non-UNIX systems and three (`argc`, `argv`, and `envp`) on UNIX. `envp` is referred to as the environment pointer and on systems where this is supported, it is set up by `_main` and passed to `main` along with `argc` and `argv`. Like `argv`, `envp` is an array of pointers to `char`.

UNIX and MS-DOS (and possibly other systems) support the notion of an environment where identifiers external to any program can be declared and assigned string values at the command-line level. The existence of these identifiers (and hence their associated values) can be detected from programs that are local to that environment. This allows arguments to be passed to programs by other than the command-line.

Environment entries are commonly used to record such information as the user's current login device and directory, the system boot device, and the name of the default print device. These entries allow programs to be written using logical devices, which can be translated into physical devices by assigning them an entry in the environment table. Multiple environment tables may exist in a hierarchy, such as `world`, `group`, and `user`, so that the scope of environment entries can be limited to a certain class of users.

Environments are not supported on all systems, and even if they are available, a particular implementation of `_main` may not pass `envp` to `main`. If an environment is supported by a system, the compiler usually supplies a run-time library function called `getenvp` (or something similar) which provides access to the table regardless of whether or not the `envp` argument to `main` is supported. (Some libraries also include a function called `putenvp` so that user programs can add new entries, and possibly delete or change others, in the environment table.)

`_main` is quite at liberty to pass as many arguments (of any type) in any order as it wants to `main` and, provided `main` contains the corresponding declarations, all such arguments can be properly accessed. Likewise, `_main` can invoke any routine that it chooses to start the user program executing. It is only by convention that `main` is the function name chosen. Of course such changes to the name of the user startup function and/or the order, type, and content of its argument list is inherently nonportable. While these changes are generally limited to adding envp to main's argument list in a hosted environment, the way in which program startup is handled in a free-standing environment is completely user-defined.

Special Command-Line Arguments

In an earlier section, the concept of redirection and pipes was discussed. Systems that do not implement these capabilities at the command-line level (such as MS-DOS version 1.x and DEC's RSX family), pass the <, >, >>, and | operators through to _main as part of the user-specified argument list. These prefixes can be detected and implemented by _main when it is setting up the argv array, in which case the arguments corresponding to them are not included in argc and argv. For example, if the argument <infile is detected, _main proceeds to use the fopen (or a similar run-time library) function to open infile as the standard input file.

The operators > and >> can be handled in a like manner. However, piping is not so simple to implement because it involves more than one program. It could be done with a small driving program that breaks piped operations into separate, single operations that it runs one after the other using temporary disk files for intermediate output/input. Because piping is performed more effectively at the operating system level, it is not normally implemented by _main.

It may be desirable to have command-line arguments that are only intended for _main and not main. One such argument that is common with MS-DOS compilers is implemented something like =nnn, where nnn is the size of the run-time stack to be created (in decimal bytes). Due to the heavy and somewhat unpredictable use of the stack in C program execution, it may be desirable to increase (or decrease) the size of the stack at run-time. If the stack is set up by _main then _main can detect and process this special argument and remove it from argc and argv before passing them to main.

Standard File Processing

The standard input and output files can often be redirected using < and > (and >>). These two files are known as stdin and stdout, respectively in C implementations. A third standard file, stderr, is used as the destination for error messages and it is typically assigned to the user's console output device.

On systems that support the notion of standard files (such as UNIX and MS-DOS version 2.x) stdin, stdout, and stderr are all opened by the operating system prior to _main's being loaded and run. In this case, these files need not be opened by _main. On systems such as MS-DOS version 1.x and DEC's RSX, these three files must be opened explicitly by _main. Of course, if redirection characters exist on the command-line, stdin and stdout are redirected accordingly before they are opened.

An array is usually defined in _main to keep track of the number and characteristics of files currently opened by the program. Each element of this array describes one open file and is usually a structure containing members such as access mode and buffer address and size. If _main explicitly opens the three stdxxx files, each will have an entry in this file table. This table is sometimes implemented using

```
struct _filetab {
    char *buffer;
    int bufsize;
        . . .
} _ftab[_MAXFILE];
```

where _MAXFILE is the maximum number of files than can be opened simultaneously. If stdin, stdout, and stderr are explicitly opened, they are traditionally allocated elements 0, 1, and 2, respectively, in _ftab. With this method, the stdxxx names are defined as follows.

```
#define stdin   (&_ftab[0]);
#define stdout  (&_ftab[1]);
#define stderr  (&_ftab[2]);
```

And the type pointer-to-file is defined using

```
#define FILE struct _filetab
```

so that when a file is successfully opened using

```
#include <stdio.h>

f()
{
    FILE *infile;

    infile = fopen("infile","r");
    . . .
}
```

`infile` actually contains the address of one of the elements in the array of structures _ftab.

The definitions of stdxxx and FILE are contained in the standard header stdio.h, which must be included if any of these are referenced. One thing to note is that the stdxxx pointers (and in fact the addresses of all _ftab entries) are constants, so these terms cannot be used as lvalues. The address of an array element becomes fixed when that array is defined, so an expression of the form

---

$$\&\_ftab[n] = (expression);$$

---

is illegal.

The macro _MAXFILE has been used to define the file pointer table size and in doing so the maximum number of simultaneously open files has also been established. The value for _MAXFILE might be 15 or 20, in which case much of the table will be empty for most applications. It was suggested above that a variable size table could be used for argv by using the malloc library function. However, this method cannot be used for _ftab because if such a table is expanded using realloc, although the contents of the old table are completely copied to the new, expanded table, the addresses to the various elements within that table may have changed, rendering any file pointers previously returned by fopen to be incorrect. So unless all open files are closed first, this method is useless. One difference between _ftab and argv is that the total contents of argv is known to _main whereas _main has no idea how many files the user program will have open at one time.

Files can be opened in either a buffered or unbuffered mode. In unbuffered mode, characters (or bytes) are physically read or written one at a time, while buffered files use line or sector input and output. While buffered I/O is much more efficient for disk and tape file processing, terminal I/O may be required to be unbuffered.

If the operating system opens the stdxxx files (and handles redirection of them), it should open them in the best mode corresponding to the device on which each resides. If _main has this task, then it must do likewise. If stdin and stdout are not redirected, they are usually set as nonbuffered.

The buffering type of any open file (including stdxxx) can be changed using the run-time library routines setbuf and setvbuf or their equivalents. Some implementations also allow the default buffering to be set globally so that it need not be explicitly specified for each new file opened unless other than the default is required.

The standard error file stderr is worth a special mention. Some systems have no provision to redirect stderr at the command-line level, so unless a file reopen function (such as freopen) is present in the library, stderr cannot be redirected. stderr is typically set to the user's output console. Although the output console may be the same destination as stdout, if stdout is redirected to a file, the stderr output will not be redirected along with it. The two are quite separate output files.

stderr is often used as follows.

```
f( )
{
    extern void error( );
    . . .
    if (i > MAX)
            error("Counter value exceeds MAX");
    . . .
}

#include <stdio.h>

int numerror = 0;
```

```
void error(message);
char *message;
{
    fprintf(stderr,"%s\n",message);
    ++numerror;
}
```

By separating error messages from stdout both outputs can be kept un-cluttered. It is preferable to have stderr unbuffered so that diagnostic output is produced as it happens. Also, if the program abnormally terminates (for example with a stack overflow) then files currently opened for write may not have their buffers flushed before they are closed, in which case the buffers' current contents are lost. Considering the purpose of stderr, output directed to it should not be lost. Of course if stderr is redirected to disk and set as unbuffered, any disk writes to it will be less efficient than if it were buffered, but because normally little is written to stderr, this is not a problem.

During program testing when error messages may be plentiful, it may be desirable to redirect stderr to a file. However, once in production, this is probably not a good idea as users would never know that any error messages were being created unless something was also written to their terminals.

If _main is responsible for opening stderr, it is remotely possible that it might encounter a problem in doing so. In this case it could not complain, because there is no error output device it can write to. Subsequently, any problems encountered by attempts to open stdin and stdout also cannot be reported. In which case it is possible for the program to terminate abruptly without any obvious reason.

Memory Partitioning and Hardware Setup

C programs can make considerable use of the stack. (Stack usage is discussed in detail in Chapter 4.) While some operating systems (such as DEC's RSX) fix the size of the stack at link-time, others allow it to be created (or changed) in _main. This generally involves initialization of the stack pointer register and several globals (such as _STKBASE and _STKSIZE), which can be accessed by the user program to detect certain characteristics of the stack, such as its base address and size.

The dynamic memory area used by the malloc family of routines is called the heap. The heap may not necessarily be set at a fixed size; it may be allocated as all the memory not used for other purposes once the stack, code, and `static` data areas have been reserved. The heap and stack may also be designed so that they share the same memory space and grow toward each other, in which case their maximum sizes are dynamic. As for the stack, heap characteristic data can be stored in globals for access by the user program.

The ability to create a stack and heap at all is dependent on the amount of physical memory available, and once the `static` data areas have been allocated there may not be enough memory left to create a required (or default) size stack or usable heap. In this case _main must terminate (hopefully with some useful message being sent to `stderr`).

On segmented memory machines (such as the Intel 8086 family) several different memory models may be supported which require the appropriate segment (or memory management) registers to be initialized by _main whenever a program is invoked.

If a `static` or `extern` pointer is not explicitly initialized, it contains the NULL pointer which "points" to location zero. Since this location is guaranteed by C never to be a valid address of an object, it is assumed that writing to that address is a bad idea. On some single-user operating systems writing to the NULL address may crash the system. Some implementations have _main create a special NULL segment or memory area that is used to hold any data written whenever the program writes through a NULL pointer. Then when the user program returns control to _main, it can check to see if this area has been modified, and if so, it can report an error (although not its location).

Floating-point operations can be performed in two basic ways; directly implemented by a floating-point processor or by emulation in software. The decision as to whether the compiler should generate in-line floating-point code or calls to emulation routines must usually be made when each source file is compiled. However, some implementations can detect the presence or absence of a floating-point processor at run-time and can take appropriate action for handling floating-point operations. Again, this can be done in _main, and if a floating-point processor is detected, it will probably also be initialized (at least for single-user systems such as the IBM PC and compatibles).

Some of the run-time library routines (most notably the math routines) can set and test a global error flag called `errno`. This global can be defined (and initialized to zero) in _main. Other global identifiers representing such values as operating system, CPU model, etc., can also be defined and initialized in _main as necessary. Obviously, the existence and possible values of such identifiers may vary from one implementation to another.

Miscellaneous _main Considerations

Global and internal static variables are guaranteed to be initialized to some given value (or zero by default) before main begins to execute. While it is common practice to initialize these variables at compile-time, some implementations may do so during program startup (in _main). The advantage of initializing these variables during startup is that the program can be restarted in memory without having to reload the executable image from disk. For ROM-based applications or other memory-resident systems, this capability is mandatory. For example, the program in a microcontroller may be reset using a switch and this requires that the program restart while remaining in memory.

In Chapter 5, several alternate implementations for the ctype.h macros are discussed, one of which uses an array called _ctype_ to record the characteristics of each character in the implementation's character set. This array may also be defined and initialized in _main.

_main is usually supplied as an object module (and possibly as source) that must be linked in with the user program objects to form an executable module. Some compilers, however, reference _main in the code generated for the source module containing the function main. In this case _main is automatically loaded from the run-time library when that module is processed by the linker.

A Smaller _main

A considerable amount of work can possibly be done by _main before control is passed to main and all this code increases the total memory (and disk) space required for the executable module. For fairly simple filters, the size of _main may exceed that of the user program code. To help keep the size of _main down, functions that force a lot of code to be included (such as printf and scanf) should not be used within _main. If the user really needs these functions, then let him pay the price by including them only if he references them in his program. If _main explicitly opens and closes the stdxxx files, the library functions fopen and fclose (or their equivalents) and any subordinate service functions are also likely to be included.

It may be desirable to have a stripped-down version of _main so that some of this space and run-time overhead can be avoided. The reason for this may be that a smaller memory (and disk) module is desired either to save space or because it won't fit in the available storage. (This occurs more frequently on floppy disk-based systems or systems with limited amounts of memory.)

Simple applications may deal only with memory-mapped data from resident data areas or with disk files, in which case they have no need for the stdxxx files. Similarly, for tasks running at an unattended network node, the applications must send all diagnostics back to a host for processing and they must perform I/O on data either from local devices/files or over the network. As such, they have no need for the standard files.

In such cases, these three files need not be opened (although they may still be by operating systems that open them prior to _main being invoked). While some applications could possibly benefit by having a smaller _main, other applications may require a different subset of _main's capabilities so it may be necessary to have several different versions. Unless you really must have a smaller _main, it may not be worth the time and the corresponding maintenance documentation effort to implement and keep track of it.

The stdxxx file capability should be removed with care, as its absence may disable command-line redirection and piping. Also, the standard error reporting mechanism cannot be used without stderr and the normal method used by _main to terminate a program may not work. (See the discussion of _exit in the next section.)

To use a smaller version of _main, the reference to _main in the linker command-line is replaced by that of the smaller version object module. For systems that automatically search the run-time library for _main, it is best to create a new version of the library in which _main is replaced by its smaller equivalent, which must have the name _main. If _main can be replaced, source code for it is usually provided along with some discussion of the implications of and procedures for modifying it.

Program Termination

A program usually is thought to terminate when the end of the main function is reached, the exit function is called, or some fatal error occurs (such as stack overflow). In all cases, control is likely to pass from somewhere inside the user program back to _main, where the program can be gracefully and predictably terminated.

Regardless of the reason a user program ends, there are a number of tasks that should be performed before control is passed back to the operating system. The buffers for all files opened for output in buffered mode should be flushed (including `stdout`). All files currently open should be properly closed so their directory entries are updated, and any temporary scratch files created by the `tmpfile` library function should be deleted. Also all system resources currently allocated should be released (if this is not automatically done by the operating system).

In any application program, it may be desirable to execute a series of functions each time the program terminates, regardless of the reason for and method of termination. Rather than insert calls to these routines in every conceivable place where the program can terminate, they can be registered (once) in a table at startup time so that they will always be executed at shutdown (in the reverse order of their registration). To register an exit processing function, use the library routine `onexit`, as follows:

```
#include <stdlib.h>

main(...)
{
    extern void f1(), f2(), f3();

    onexit(f3);
    onexit(f2);
    onexit(f1);
    ...
}
```

When _main regains control, it will invoke the exit service functions in the order f1, f2, and f3. These functions must not have any arguments and they must be of type `void` (they cannot have a return value). The same exit function should not be registered more than once. These service routines execute after the user program code has terminated, so they only have access to global variables or variables local to _main. Pointers to any `auto` variables within the user program will be very unreliable, although pointers to any `static` data should be usable.

There are three possible ways to terminate `main` in a normal manner. They are

---

```
1.  return;
2.  falling through the closing brace '}'
3.  return(n);
```

Methods 1 and 2 are identical; both result in an undefined value being returned to _main, whereas method 3 specifically indicates what that return value is. Function main has a return type of int, so when it returns control to _main, its return value may be used to control further processing.

If _main contains code like

```
#define MXCMDARG 32

_main(...)
{
    int argc;
    char *argv[MXCMDARG];
    ...
    exit(main(argc,argv));
}
```

---

then a problem can exist. If either of the return methods 1 and 2 above are used then some garbage int value is returned and _main cannot distinguish it from any valid value that could be returned by method 3. This return value is then passed through to the exit function which passes it back to the calling environment. The whole purpose of having an exit code (as produced by exit) is so that it can be interrogated by the calling environment to check on the success or failure of the user program. Clearly, if either method 1 or 2 is used to terminate main, the exit code will be bogus.

Because _main can never guarantee that the value returned from main is real, implementations often resort to the following termination approach.

```
#define MXCMDARG 32

_main(...)
```

```
{
    int argc;
    char *argv[MXCMDARG];
    . . .
    main(argc,argv);
    exit(0);
}
```

Here, the return value from main is ignored and the program always terminates with an exit code of zero (signifying success). In this case, if programmers really want a nonzero exit code, they must use exit(n); from main (or some other function) instead of return(n);. However, the fact remains that return(n); is a perfectly legitimate statement in main except that in some implementations it may be ignored.

The exit library function can be used to abnormally (or normally) terminate a C program. It is used as follows.

```
#include <stdlib.h>

f()
{
    if (condition)
            exit(n);
}
```

When exit is called, it runs the functions registered via onexit, output file buffers are flushed, all open files are closed, and temporary files are deleted. Whether or not the termination is considered normal or abnormal is purely a matter of the value of the argument n. Typically, an exit value of zero means successful termination. exit performs exactly the same tasks regardless of this value. If you plan to attach meaning to exit code values for a particular program, you must always terminate that program using exit.

If an abbreviated version of _main is used for program startup, then a corresponding abbreviated version of exit may be needed. For example, if the new _main does not open the stdxxx files then exit need not close them. Some implementations supply a library routine called _exit for this purpose. (The effect of using exit with a customized version of _main, is implementation-defined.)

It is possible to truly terminate a program in an abnormal fashion, by using the abort library function. In this case, the normal shutdown tasks performed by exit may or may not be done depending on the implementation. The abort function may result in the the kill library function being invoked, which in turn causes the program's calling environment to abort the user program.

Implementations that use a stack may provide a compiler option for stack overflow detection. If the option is selected then each time code is generated that uses the stack (such as function call argument lists and auto variable allocation) code will also be generated to see if there is sufficient room on the stack for the new data. If there is not, then the program traps to some service handler which terminates the program in a controlled manner. This handler may reside in _main and it is generally reached by an unconditional jump, since it can never return control. Also, it can never be invoked as a subroutine, as this would require stack space, which of course does not exist.

The addition of stack checking code both increases the size of the executable module and the time it takes to execute, but without it a stack overflow error may result in corrupted static data or heap, or even overwritten program code, depending on how the stack is implemented. Once a program has been tested for a long period and most of its normal logic paths have been exercised, then it may be desirable to remove this extra checking code (if possible).

The X3J11 Draft

A number of points regarding program startup and termination in the proposed ANSI Standard are worth mentioning. They are:

- A freestanding environment can invoke a program in any way it sees fit. It does not have to begin with main, nor does the starting module have to be of type int or have the arguments argc and argv. The whole process is strictly programmer-defined. A number of criteria must be satisfied by hosted environments, including the fact that they must supply a run-time library that contains at least *all* of the functions defined in the standard. A compiler *cannot* implement a subset of this library and still be conforming. A number of other considerations for a hosted environment are discussed individually below.

- A return from the initial call to main must be equivalent to

```
exit(main(argc, argv));
```

in which case if main is terminated using return; (without a return value) or by falling through the outermost closing brace, an unpredictable exit code results. This problem was discussed above in the section on Program Termination.

- main may have zero or two arguments declared. The type and purpose of any extra arguments (e.g., envp) is implementation-defined.

- The arguments argc and argv and the strings pointed to by argv must be able to be modified by the user program. Their contents must not be changed by the host environment or startup code once main has been invoked.

- If argv[0] is not supplied by the host environment, it must point to a string that has '\0' as its first character.

- argv[argc] must be a NULL pointer. This allows the end of the argv array to be detected if it is processed without using argc.

- If the host environment cannot supply argv strings with both upper- and lower-case alphabetic characters, it must supply them in lower case.

- The Standard does not require that quoted command-line arguments be acceptable for specifying arguments with embedded white-space. Whether or not this feature is supported is implementation-defined.

- If possible, stderr is to be opened in an unbuffered mode. stdout is to be opened in a fully buffered mode if and only if it is not directed to a terminal-type device. The setbuf and setvbuf library functions can be used to explicitly set a file buffering mode; a number of predefined macros exist in stdio.h to help with this process. The library function freopen is provided to allow stderr (or any other file) to be reopened which affectively allows that file to be redirected.

- An implementation must support text files with records containing at least 254 characters (including the terminating newline character). The value of BUFSIZ (the buffer size used by setbuf) must be at least 256.

- SYS_OPEN is an integral constant expression that represents the number of files the implementation guarantees can be open simultaneously. It is defined in stdio.h and it must be at least 8, including the three stdxxx files.

- The onexit function must allow the registration of at least thirty two functions.

- The global int errno (as declared in stddef.h) may be used by certain library functions to provide error information. The description of each function that sets this variable should indicate the value(s) used and their meaning(s).

- The void function type has been added to the language so that functions need not have a return value and if they are declared to be of type void then the compiler can detect if they try to return a value or if their caller tries to use a returned value. The lesson, then is to use void when you really mean it and some other type when you really mean that. Function main must be declared as type int, it cannot be type void.

CHAPTER 7

The Run-Time Library

C is touted as a widely portable language, and with the proper discipline and management, it can be. Whenever the term "the C Language" is used, it refers not only to the language definition, but also to the preprocessor and run-time library. The preprocessor is very simple and leaves little room for extensions or variant and incompatible implementations. The language definition consists of three categories: those capabilities absolutely guaranteed to be in the language and which behave as specified, those things that are implementation-defined, and those that are undefined. All three categories can significantly impact program portability—the first because there is no common agreement to the contents of this class, and the second and third because of their inherent properties.

As anyone who has ported a nontrivial amount of C code can attest, the biggest portability stumbling block is usually the run-time library. Here, problems arise for several reasons; the same function is not available in both libraries, the required function is available but by a different name and argument list format, the same named function has a different argument list and/or behaves slightly differently, or user-written function names conflict with new library functions.

The proposed ANSI Standard on C addresses the preprocessor, language, and library definitions, and besides identifying the exact contents and behavior of a conforming C implementation, the Standard identifies those aspects deemed to be implementation-defined or undefined.

Until the proposed Standard is in force *and* conforming implementations of it are made available, there will be no such thing as "the Standard Library." Various compilers claim K&R conformance, UNIX Version 7 or System V conformance, etc. However, each such standard has its own idiosyncrasies. In the absence of a reasonable and common definition of the library, the basis for this chapter will be the ANSI X3J11 Draft Standard as of November 1985, making the format of this chapter different from that used in all other chapters.

The argument for a standard library (and language) definition is often given as "the concern for portability." However, the amount of C code that may actually need to be written portably is considerably less than that designed to run in only a single environment. Perhaps a more important consideration is programmer portability; the ability for one programmer to move from one C environment to another without having to learn a new language or library.

General Library Considerations

One of the most significant aspects of the proposed Standard is that a conforming hosted C implementation *must* provide a run-time library that includes at least all of the specified capabilities. Freestanding implementations (those that run without the benefit of an operating system) can provide whatever library capability they desire (including none).

Each library function is declared in a standard header, but whereas traditionally stdio.h has contained more or less everything for a given implementation, this is no longer true. A whole series of (possibly) new standard headers has been introduced, meaning that existing code that referenced only stdio.h may now need to include other headers. For example, the string manipulation functions (such as strcpy and strcmp) are now declared in string.h.

Even though most programs use only a few of the standard headers, the names of functions and macros referenced in those unused headers are still reserved. For example, the header time.h defines the macro time_t and declares the function clock (among other things). If a program does not include time.h then it could use either time_t or clock as local identifiers without conflict. However, this program would not be a conforming one. Library macros and functions are globally reserved regardless of whether or not they are used. The names of the new headers and the macros and functions they contain are listed in Appendix A.

All external identifiers that begin with an underscore are reserved. An implementation may define macros whose name begins with two or more underscores.

The standard library defines a set of macros and functions. Some of the library capabilities must be implemented as macros (e.g., va_arg in stdarg.h), others must be implemented as functions (e.g., fputc in stdio.h) and yet others may be implemented as either. If you desire to get at a real function, you may use #undef to remove an existing macro definition by the same name. Of course, this requires that a function by that name exist in the library and that it performs the same job as the removed macro. Removing macros for this reason should be done with extreme care and may result in nonportable code. Unless you are absolutely sure that a function is being invoked, don't use arguments with unary operators that generate side affects (e.g., + + and − −).

Several pseudo types have been introduced in the standard headers to help with portability. They are size_t and ptrdiff_t. size_t is the integral type of the result of the sizeof operator. Quite possibly size_t is defined using

```
typedef unsigned int size_t;
```

A number of library functions have an argument of type size_t. For example:

```
void *calloc(size_t int nelem, size_t elsize);
void *malloc(size_t size);
void *realloc(void *ptr, size_t size);
```

In each of the three memory allocation functions the required memory size must be stated in terms of size_t. (The format used to declare these function types and argument lists is that adopted by function prototypes, which are discussed below). Several functions also return values of type size_t. The most notable of these is strlen.

```
size_t strlen(const char *s);
size_t strcspn(const char *s1, const char *s2);
size_t strspn(const char *s1, const char *s2);
```

197

Pointer arithmetic can involve the subtraction of two pointers and the type of the result of such a subtraction is ptrdiff_t. For example,

```
#include <stddef.h>

f()
{
    ptrdiff_t pdiff;
    double da[100];
    double *dp1 = da[25];
    double *dp2 = da[95];

    pdiff = dp2 - dp1;
}
```

The standard header time.h includes the types clock_t and time_t, both of which are arithmetic types capable of representing times suitable for use by the library functions clock and time. They are used as follows:

```
clock_t clock(void);
time_t time(time_t *timer);
```

The concept of a pointer to void has been introduced to deal with situations in which a generic pointer was required or returned, as for the following memory allocation functions.

```
void *calloc(size_t int nelem, size_t elsize);
void *malloc(size_t size);
void *realloc(void *ptr, size_t size);
```

Traditionally these functions have been declared to return pointers to char and these pointers had to be cast into the required pointer type if other than pointer to char was required. While pointers to void still need to be cast in this way, a method now exists for labelling generic pointers. Pointers to void have the interesting property that they satisfy all possible alignment requirements for a particular implementation, and this is a necessity for the above memory allocation functions. Pointers to void have absolutely nothing to do with the void function type.

Some functions require (void *) arguments, return them, or both. For example:

```
int fread(void *ptr, size_t size, size_t nelem,
        FILE *stream);
void *memcpy(void *sl, const void *s2, size_t n);
void *memset(void *s, int c, size_t n);
```

To properly use the memcpy function, use something like

```
#include <string.h>

f()
{
    int *pil, *pi2;

    /* initialize pil, pi2 somehow */

    memcpy((void *) pil, (void *) pi2,
            sizeof(int) * 100);
}
```

Here, pil and pi2 are both pointers to ints, and while it is certainly possible on many implementations that these could directly be used as arguments to memcpy, this approach is not maximally portable. It is possible (and likely) that on new machines (and possibly some existing ones) that pointers to different types of objects will have different sizes. So by explicitly casting the pointer to int argument to a pointer to void, it is guaranteed that the argument will be interpreted exactly as was intended. Any necessary conversion done because of the (possibly) different size of int and void pointers will be performed. On a machine where different pointer sizes exist, the pointer to int might otherwise be misinterpreted by memcpy.

The macro NULL is often used in C programs and it is typically defined by

---

```
#define NULL 0
```

---

or

```
#define NULL 0L
```

---

depending on the relationship between int and pointer size for a particular machine. In any case, this conditional approach can cause some portability problems when pointers are compared with NULL or when the NULL pointer is passed as an argument in place of a pointer variable or expression. The new definition of NULL includes a third possibility, namely

---

```
#define NULL ((void *) 0)
```

---

where the integer zero is cast to type pointer to void. Pointer to void can safely be compared with any other pointer type and pointers of any type can be safely converted to pointer to void without any loss of precision.

This change may slow existing code down if that code already casts NULL into some other type, as the new definition will just add another explicit conversion. Depending on the existing cast and the host architecture, it is possible that the code will not run correctly without modification (perhaps by removing the programmer's explicit cast).

A global variable called errno is declared in stddef.h and it is used by a number of library functions to return an error code. errno is an lvalue that designates a volatile int. (The volatile type modifier has been added to the language to identify memory locations that can be altered by means other than in the current program. They may be memory-mapped locations such as device registers or I/O ports.) A value of zero in errno indicates no error, and a positive value indicates an error. Although errno is set to zero at program startup, a user program should always set errno to zero before invoking a library function that may set it. For example,

```
#include <stddef.h>
#include <stdio.h>
#include <math.h>

f()
{
    double result;
    double value;

    value = −45.5;

    errno = 0;
    result = sqrt(value);
    if (errno == EDOM)
            puts("Domain error on sqrt arg");
}
```

A domain error occurs if sqrt is given a negative argument and all domain errors detected in the math.h functions cause error to be set to the macro EDOM defined in math.h. (The value actually returned by sqrt for a domain error is zero, although this cannot be used to detect a domain error as it is a legitimate return value.)

Function Prototypes

Several references have been made to prototypes in previous chapters. As the name might suggest, a prototype is the skeletal declaration of a function. Specifically, this declaration contains the function's return type and the list and types of valid arguments for that function. For example, the prototype declarations for some of the functions declared in ctype.h are

```
int islower(int c);
int isprint(int c);
int ispunct(int c);
int isspace(int c);
int isupper(int c);
```

Each declaration indicates that the functions return an int and that they each have one int argument. Note also that the declaration is terminated with a semicolon. Except for the fact that there is no function body (within { . . . }), a function prototype looks just like a function definition (hence the name prototype).

A primary purpose of prototypes is to allow argument list type, order, and count checking across multiple source files. If the prototype for a function is placed in a header that is included in the file where that function is defined and in all files where it is referenced, the compiler can check that all references to the same function match each other and that of the definition.

Other examples of prototypes (from stdio.h) are

```
int remove(const char *pathname);
int rename(const char *old, const char *new);
FILE *fopen(const char *pathname,
        const char *type);
void setbuf(FILE *stream, char *buf);
```

In some of these prototypes (and others shown above) the new keyword const is used. This indicates that the corresponding variables are to remain constant; they may not be changed by the user code. Consider the following library prototypes.

```
char *strcpy(char *s1, const char *s2);
char *strcat(char *s1, const char *s2);
```

The second argument to both strcpy and strcat has a type modifier of const. Therefore, these functions are prohibited from modifying these arguments. If within strcpy or strcat, s2 were used as an lvalue, the compiler would issue a diagnostic. Of course, variables other than those used as function arguments can be declared const. For example,

```
f()
{
    const long = 12345;
    static const struct st {
            int i;
            char ca[4];
    } sl = {25,"abc"};
}
```

The prototype naming conventions also allow for the specification of the leading part of an argument list. The most likely use of this is with functions that have a variable number of arguments.

```
int printf(const char *format, ...);
int scanf(const char *format, ...);
```

Here, all of the known (guaranteed) argument types are declared and this list is followed by a comma and an ellipsis indicating that there may be more arguments but no information is known about their type or number. This format can also be used with fixed type and size argument lists but it serves no purpose and, in fact, reduces the ability of the compiler to diagnose argument list mismatches.

If a prototype is declared without an argument list such as in

```
int function();
```

then no information is known about the argument list, so the compiler can not perform checking. To indicate that a function has no arguments, the format

```
int function(void);
```

should be used instead. (The new keyword void has three possible uses; as a function type, a pointer type, and in function prototypes.)

Given that the prototype for strcpy is

```
char *strcpy(char *s1, const char *s2);
```

one might expect that the actual definition of strcpy would be something like

```
char *strcpy(s1, s2)
char *s1;
const char *s2;
{
    . . .
}
```

While this format would be correct, it is deprecated by the Standard. Deprecated features are those which are approved begrudgingly and may not be supported by future revisions of the Standard. Deprecated features are often those which are currently common practice but for which an alternate (replacement) mechanism has been provided. Programmers who have a strong incentive to write conforming programs should replace function definitions such as this with

```
char *strcpy(char *s1, const char *s2)
{
    . . .
}
```

Similarly, the use of function declarations without argument lists as for function() above, is deprecated requiring that the special identifier void be used to ensure conformance.

Another benefit of prototypes is that they may be used to bypass the default widening rules on function arguments. (Whether or not a prototype allows the default widening rules to be overridden, is implementation-defined.)

```
f()
{
    extern void g();
    char c;
    short s;
    float f;

    . . .
    g(c, s, f);
}
```

c and s are widened to int and f to double before being passed to g. In function g, the definition would normally be

```
void g(c, s, f)
char c;
short s;
float f;
{
    . . .
}
```

However, if the prototype

```
void g(char c, short s, float f);
```

were used, the default argument widening rules would be bypassed allowing the conversion overhead to be omitted. This is of particular use to programmers who use `float` instead of `double`. They no longer need to pay the price of `float`/`double`/`float` conversions. (Note that the current `math.h` routines still require `double` arguments though.) Also an implementation can perform floating-point arithmetic in `float` precision if it can determine that `double` is not necessary.

While it can be messy, it is possible to have some arguments in a list widened while others in that same list are not, by using the ellipsis specifier. The ellipsis notation causes argument type checking to cease such that any arguments that actually follow will go unchecked. These unchecked arguments are widened as if no prototype were currently in scope.

All of the prototypes shown above have variables declared along with each argument type. These variables have prototype scope that ends at the semicolon terminator. They are formal argument names only and have no storage space or name-space.

`ctype.h`

This header declares a number of functions that are useful for testing and converting characters. (The possibility of implementing these functions as macros was discussed in Chapter 9.)

The functions are of the form

```
int isalnum(int c);
int isalpha(int c);
```

where the int c must be representable in an unsigned char or must equal the value EOF (typically -1). If c has any other value, the behavior is undefined.

The character constant '\v' has been added to the language and represents a vertical tab. It is treated as white-space by the isspace function.

math.h

This header contains the three macros EDOM, ERANGE, and HUGE_VAL. The first two expand to nonzero integral constant expressions, while the HUGE_VAL expands to a positive double expression. These macros are used to indicate the existence of a domain or range error using errno. (errno was discussed earlier in this Chapter.)

For a domain error, errno is set to the value of EDOM and the function returns a value (as specified for each function). A range error causes errno to be set to the value ERANGE and the function returns zero if the result underflows. If the result overflows, the function returns HUGE_VAL with the same sign as the correct value would have had.

```
#include <stddef.h>
#include <stdio.h>
#include <math.h>

f()
{
    double result, x, y;

    . . .
    errno = 0;
    result = pow(x, y);
    if (errno == EDOM)
            puts("Domain error on pow arg");
    else if (errno == ERANGE)
            puts("Range error on pow arg");
    . . .
}
```

Numerical analysts may make heavy use of the math routines and as such would be interested in domain and range errors. However, the method used above for detecting and reporting these errors is verbose and a more compact and less error-prone mechanism is preferred.

```
#include <stddef.h>
#include <math.h>

double vdomrang(double retcode, const char *message);

f()
{
    double result, x, y;

    ...
    errno = 0;
    result = vdomrang(pow(x, y), "f:pow");
    ...
}
```

```
#include <stddef.h>
#include <math.h>
#define UNKNOWER 0
#define DOMAINER 1
#define RANGEER 2

double vdomrang(double retcode, const char *message)
{
    if (errno == EDOM)
            domraner(DOMAINER,message);
    else if (errno == ERANGE)
            domraner(RANGEER,message);
    else
            domraner(UNKNOWER,message);

    return (retcode);
}
```

Rather than handle domain and range checking in-line, this is done by the routine vdomrang (validate domain and range). The return value from pow is passed to vdomrang, which passes it straight back as its return value. The second argument to vdomrang is a string containing a locator for a possible error message such as function name and math function name. If a domain or range error is detected, this message is displayed by domraner along with either a domain or range identifier. The function domraner may display this information on a screen or printer or it may send it to some other node if it is running at an unattended network node (as is often used in process control applications).

The object here is to implement a general-purpose math error handler so that once that handler has been written, the application programmer is not burdened with coding the error checking for each math function call.

The above technique could have been implemented as

```
      . . .
result = pow(x, y);
vdomrang("f:pow");
      . . .
```

which allows vdomrang to have only one argument although this method is more prone to the programmer forgetting to add the error checking call, whereas the first approach has it embedded as part of the math routine call. Either way, the end result is still the same.

Such common error checking can work well with the math functions since most of them return a double value. However, not all of these functions can detect a domain or range error. For example, fabs returns the absolute value of a double number. No domain or range error is possible, so it would be pointless to use

```
result = vdomrang(fabs(x), "x:fabs");
```

for this function. Since vdomrang should never find an error, there is no point in wasting time by calling it. Actually, fabs should *not* be validated by this method because it *is* possible that vdomrang will report an error even though one does not actually exist as a result of using fabs. This is possible because of the definition of errno.

The value of errno may be set to nonzero (indicating an error) by a library function call *even* if there is *no* error, provided the use of errno is not documented for that function. So, as the Standard does not declare that fabs explicitly sets errno, it can be assumed that, for whatever perverted reason, it might actually do so, in which case a bogus error would be reported.

As mentioned above in the discussion of prototypes, float arguments can be passed to user functions without being widened, but not to math library routines because the prototypes for the latter declare the arguments and return values (for almost all functions) to be type double. Unless you have float versions of these library routines, the float/double/float conversion overhead that results from calling them will still exist. To allow for future expansion in this area, the Standard has reserved the math library function names with a suffix of f and l. This allows a future version of the Standard to add float and long double versions of these routines without breaking conforming programs.

signal.h

This header defines macros and declares functions that are used to handle various signals. Such signals are often termed *Interrupts,* or *Synchronous* (or *Asynchronous*) *System Traps.*

The signal function can be used to define the type of processing that is to occur when a specified type of signal is detected. A signal can be passed off to a default handler as defined by the implementation, it can be processed by a user-specified routine, or it can be ignored. To select one of these three options, the appropriate function pointer is used as the second argument to signal. The macros SIG_IGN and SIG_DFL expand to constant expressions suitable for use as this second argument and they indicate "ignore signal" and "default signal processing", respectively.

Because the second argument is a pointer to a handler function, these two macro expressions must be such that they can be differentiated from a real user-declared function, and it is the implementer's responsibility to define them as such. The values of these two macro expressions cannot be the address of a legitimate user function, otherwise signal could not distinguish them.

Several other macros are defined in `signal.h` and their names all begin with the prefix `SIG`. They are used to identify the specific signal to be recognized. Currently, only five or six signal types are defined in this manner, but to allow for future expansion of this list, the prefix `SIG` is reserved.

Just how useful can a standard signal handler be? A standard cannot hope to cater to all existing (let alone future) types of signals, so the problem reduces to identifying that small list of signals that the vast majority of reasonable architectures can or do implement. Of course, implementers are at liberty to add extensions to this list, as no doubt they will.

Consider a specific example of signal processing using a DEC PDP-11 processor running one of the RSX-11 family of operating systems. This type of configuration is quite commonly used in real-time, process control applications and is well suited to programs being written in C (with an appropriate dose of assembler). Such a system may also be implemented as a distributed network with processors on the workshop floor without any peripherals except analog and digital I/O devices and a network communications link. All signals detected in any of these remote nodes must be totally processed by the machine on which they occur and these machines must recover from these signals wherever possible.

When numeric data is being read from an input measuring, counting, or integrating device, it is quite possible to get bogus values even after a significant amount of filtering and eventually these can result in a floating-point-type exception, such as zero divide or overflow. The signal generated causes a handler to be invoked which may ignore the whole calculation and go to the next one, or it may substitute a default value, or it may use some function of the previous measurement(s). In any case, the handler must be able to recover in time to handle the next set of incoming data.

The standard macro `SIGFPE` is defined as the signal type for floating-point exceptions, but this category may be way too coarse as it lumps all such signals into one when, in fact, the programmer may wish to distinguish between them. Also, certain math errors, such as integer overflow (and underflow) and integer divide by zero, may not be detectable by the host machine, in which case no signal is generated by them. Other errors, such as taking the square root of a negative number cause `sqrt` to set a domain error. Whether or not a signal is generated is undefined.

By its very nature, signal handling is implementation dependent, particularly on machines such as the PDP-11 (with RSX-11), whose whole business is that of dealing with real-time events. Therefore, these systems have a very complex and sophisticated signal generation and handling environment builtin and come complete with a library of software to detect and process those signals. C run-time libraries implemented on RSX-11 (and DEC's VAX/VMS) quite likely invoke the operating system run-time library to perform signal handling on their behalf, and these libraries are certain to be reentrant.

The functions in the Standard library are not guaranteed to be reentrant and, as such, they should not be used by a handler that returns control to the user program. This can be a severe limitation on signal processing because, in many cases, control must be regained after processing signals such as floating-point exceptions.

An implementer wishing to conform to the Standard must supply the signal handling capabilities as defined, but whether or not they extend them to fully handle the underlying architecture or just simply supply a set of separate library routines outside of the Standard recommended mechanism is up to them. The end result may be that the signal handling functions and macros defined in the Standard will be implemented in their crudest form just to get Standard conformance, while the real signal handling mechanism will use some other means (and one which does not contradict the Standard definition). The idea of writing nontrivial signal handling code in a portable fashion is suspect at best because such an implementation cannot take full advantage of the signal generation and detection mechanisms provided by the underlying hardware and operating system.

One possible use for portable signal handling is that of detecting and servicing special keyboard sequences such as `break` and `Control/C`.

`stdio.h`

This header contains macro definitions and function declarations that can be used to perform input and output. (Although `sprintf` and `sscanf` don't strictly perform I/O, logically they are part of the `printf` and `scanf` I/O family).

A major difference between C and other high-level languages is that in C, the I/O mechanism is not part of the language. Instead, this function is performed by a set of routines defined in the run-time library (and declared in `stdio.h`). This approach has advantages and disadvantages.

By making the I/O external, the language definition can be simpler and less dependent on its operational environment because the I/O is relegated to the run-time library. This approach also allows users to replace a library routine with a leaner or faster version of their own. (Of course, this may affect program portability.)

On the negative side, the compiler is completely ignorant about functions such as `printf` and `scanf`. To it, these functions look like any other C function and no special treatment is given them. In particular, their argument lists are not inspected for compatibility with the edit mask string, the edit masks are not checked for validity, and the arguments to `scanf` are not verified as being addresses. Even if edit mask checking were done, this would probably be limited to string literal masks only. But the mask could be specified as a pointer to `char` whose value is only known at run-time, or the edit mask could be created dynamically at run-time. Both capabilities would be severely restricted (if not prohibited) if I/O were part of the language.

For the most part, the problems just mentioned are being solved by debugging utilities such as `lint` and other run-time analyzers. In any case, programmers used to writing in assembler are familiar with performing I/O via macros or subroutine calls, so they should have little difficulty in adjusting to this feature of C. On the other hand, high-level language programmers used to having I/O statements in the language, may need to make a psychological adjustment.

There are two primary methods used to terminate records in sequential files. UNIX-like systems use a line feed (LF) only, while non-UNIX systems largely use a carriage return/line feed (CR/LF) pair. (Some systems may actually start a record with a LF and end it with a CR rather than just by ending it a CR/LF.) This problem should largely (if not totally) be solved in the library, provided of course that the library is a conforming one, and will not be discussed here. The record terminator problem can undoubtedly be a problem when porting existing code between UNIX and non-UNIX systems.

`stdio.h` contains a number of macro definitions. They include expressions for use in `setvbuf`, `setbuf`, and `fseek` file positioning. The FILE macro and the standard I/O stream macros `stdin`, `stdout`, and `stderr` are discussed in Chapter 9, as is SYS_OPEN, the number of simultaneously open files allowed. The macro EOF expands to a negative integral constant expression that is used to indicate end-of-file. It may be returned by a number of library input functions. Note that the Standard does not specify an actual negative value, so that existing values other than the traditional -1 can still be accommodated. EOF is typically defined using

```
#define EOF (-1)
```

The setbuf and setvbuf functions can be used to specify the type of buffering to be used for a file. Possible types are unbuffered, line buffered, and fully buffered. Default file buffering (particularly for the standard files) is discussed in Chapter 9.

The printf **Function**

Perhaps the most used library function, at least in terms of C programming examples in books and documentation, is printf. While the printf family (printf, fprintf, and sprint) are easy to use and moderately powerful, they can be the source of hard-to-find bugs and they pull in large quantities of code as service routines, which most times are not required. Despite its negative points, printf is useful and is worth some special mention. Unless otherwise stated, all references to printf will include the printf family.

The format of a conversion specifier (or edit mask) is

%[flag][width][precision][modifier]type

As shown, all parts except the leading % character and the trailing type specifier are optional.

The flag character can be one of four possible values; '-', '+', '#', or a space. In the past, a flag of '0' was also permitted and it was used to get leading zero padding rather than space padding. This method is deprecated by the Standard and it can be achieved via the precision specifier.

Using leading zeros with negative values will give strange results, as follows:

```
#include <stdio.h>

main()
{
    int i;
```

```
    for (i = -3; i <= 3; ++i)
            printf("[%3d] [%03d]\n",i,i);

}
```

```
[  -3] [0-3]
[  -2] [0-2]
[  -1] [0-1]
[   0] [000]
[   1] [001]
[   2] [002]
[   3] [003]
```

The '-' flag indicates that the field should be left-justified within the given width. If no width is present, or if the size of the value exceeds the specified minimum field width, the '-' flag is ignored. The '+' flag causes a leading plus or minus sign to be used, provided the value to be printed is signed. A space flag causes a signed value to have either a leading space (if it is positive) or a leading minus sign (if it is negative).

The '#' flag indicates that some alternate form of presentation is to be used. When used with %o and %x (or %X) it forces a leading zero and "0x" (or "0X") to be used. For octal zero, only one zero is produced not "00". Likewise, hexadecimal zero appears as "0" not "0x0". For floating-point masks, the decimal point will always appear even if no fractional digits follow and for the %g (and %G) masks, trailing zeros will be present.

The field width is a minimum value, not a maximum as used in other languages. This means that rather than get some field overflow value like "*****" in various implementations of FORTRAN, the whole value is displayed if the value exceeds the field size. While this may cause a columnar report to be misaligned, it does at least display the actual value, making problem detection easier.

The precision specifier has the form ".n", where n is an integer that controls the precision depending on the value type being converted. If n is omitted, a value of zero is assumed and if both precision and minimum field width are specified, the precision is used to determine the padding size. For numeric values, the converted value will have leading zeros if necessary to satisfy the precision given (and this method should be used instead of the '0' flag). A precision of zero causes a zero value to appear as a space - it causes zero suppression.

A negative width is interpreted as a '-' flag and positive width, while a negative precision is ignored. Either or both the width and field specifiers can be '*', in which case, their value is taken from an int argument. For example:

```c
#include <stdio.h>

f()
{
    int width, precisn;
    double dval;

    width = ...
    precisn = ...
    dval = ...
    printf("%*.*f\n",width,precisn,dval);
    printf("%*.3f\n",width,dval);
    printf("%10.*f\n",precisn,dval);
}
```

This format allows the width and/or precision to be calculated at run-time, providing more flexibility. One example of using '*' is in dealing with code that is to be ported across 16- and 32-bit systems, where the size of an int is 16 and 32 bits respectively and a byte contains 8 bits. In the code int values are to be displayed in hexadecimal format with leading zeros. A 16-bit int requires 4 hex digits and a 32-bit int requires 8, so the precision needs to be dynamically specified.

```c
#include <stdio.h>

f()
{
    int i;

    i = ...
    precisn = sizeof(int) * 2;

    printf("%.*x\n",precisn,i);
}
```

This results in precisn being either 4 or 8, which is used as the minimum number of digits to appear (effectively, it gives the width), and if the value can be converted using less than this, leading zeros are added.

The modifier, if present, may be one of 'h', 'l', or 'L'. The 'h' modifier is used with integral types to indicate an argument is a short int, 'l' is likewise used to indicate long int, and 'L' is used with the floating point types to indicate the new variable type long double. Note that %lf (implying long float) can no longer be used as a synonym for double. If a modifier other than 'h', 'l', or 'L' appears, it is ignored.

A number of changes and enhancements have occurred regarding the type specifiers. For example, both %x and %X can be used for hexadecimal conversion. The former uses the characters "abcdef" in displays, while the latter uses "ABCDEF". Likewise, both %e and %g have new forms %E and %G. The upper-case versions cause the 'e' in the exponent display to be 'E'. Exponents will always contain at least two digits.

The mask %p has been added to convert pointers to an implementation-defined sequence of printable characters. Pointer values written out using printf can be input by scanf using the same mask. The argument corresponding to %p is assumed to be a pointer to void.

The %n mask is new and it is also quite different in that it causes information to be stored in one of printf's arguments rather than taken from it. Specifically, this mask causes the number of characters written to the output stream thus far by this particular call to printf to be stored in the int pointed to by the corresponding argument.

```
#include <stdio.h>

char *name;
int reclen;

printf("Name: %s%n\n",name,&reclen);
```

In this example, text and a string variable are written to stdout and the number of characters written is stored in reclen. Note that reclen must be passed by address so that it can be modified by printf. In this case, the terminating '\n' is not included in the count. The length of a string may vary, so it might be useful to get that length back each time it is printed. (Of course, `strlen` could be used instead.)

```
#include <stdio.h>

char *s1, *s2;
int len1, len2, lenstr;

printf("%s%n%s%n\n",s1,&len1,s2,&len2);
lenstr = len2 - len1;
```

In this example the length of s2 is calculated, and while this length should exactly correspond to the number of characters written by `printf`, what happens if s2 contains character constants like `'\v'`, `'\t'` and `'\n'`? Many modern operating systems use device drivers or handlers to actually perform physical I/O, and depending on the device being used, there may be some logical-to-physical character translation involved. For example, a `'\n'` might be converted to a CR/LF pair on output, a `'\v'` or `'\f'` might be converted to a series of CR/LF and a `'\t'` may be converted to a series of spaces if the output device does not support hardware tabbing. These conversions will be transparent to `printf`, but if they do take place, the number of characters physically written may differ from those logically written by `printf`, so the value obtained by using %n should be used with care when other than normal printable characters are involved.

The mask %i is now a synonym for %d.

The generic format of a mask is %? where ? can be any one of 'c', 'd', 'e', 'E', 'f', 'g', 'G', 'i', 'n', 'o', 'p', 's', 'u', 'x', 'X', or '%'. (%% causes a percent symbol to be written.) If the conversion character following the % is a lower-case letter not in this list, the behavior is undefined. (In fact, these lower-case letters are reserved for future use by the Standard.) If the conversion character is any other than those mentioned above, the behavior is implementation-defined. These rules are slightly different from those stated in K&R where any character following a % is displayed if it is not a recognized conversion character. For example, %a and %# would cause 'a' and '#' to be written out.

Occasionally it is useful to be able to display values using a binary radix and, as `printf` does not support such a mask, you will need to write your own facility. The following program is not terribly elegant but it does the job. By using `sizeof`, it could be made word-size independent.

```
/* A 16-bit word-to-binary display */

#include <stdio.h>

struct mask {
    unsigned hi_bit : 1;
    unsigned        : 15;
};

union {
    struct mask word;
    int i;
} u;

main()
{
    int i, j;

    for (i = -30; i <= 30; i += 10) {
            printf("i = %3d (dec), ",i);
            u.i = i;
            j = 16;
            while (j--) {
                    printf("%d",u.word.hi_bit);
                    u.i <<= 1;
            }
            puts(" (bin)");
    }
}


i = -30 (dec),   1111111111100010 (bin)
i = -20 (dec),   1111111111101100 (bin)
i = -10 (dec),   1111111111110110 (bin)
i =   0 (dec),   0000000000000000 (bin)
i =  10 (dec),   0000000000001010 (bin)
i =  20 (dec),   0000000000010100 (bin)
i =  30 (dec),   0000000000011110 (bin)
```

Using the flag characters, width, precision, and padding, it is possible to get reasonable commercial edit masks, although many of those in COBOL PICTURE clauses and FORTRAN-77 FORMAT statements can not be directly implemented with printf. Trailing sign or CR/DB (credit/debit) could be printed as a string that is passed as an argument using the conditional operator.

```
printf("%10d %s\n",val,(val < 0) ? "-" : "+");
```

However, this method would not remove the leading minus sign from negative values. For commercial-data displays, it is quite likely you will have to write custom formatting routines. (You could use sprintf and modify the output buffer before printing it.)

Function prototypes were discussed earlier in this chapter and these include a convention for handling variable argument lists as used by printf (and scanf). No argument list checking is possible when this "..." ellipsis format is used. The stdargs.h standard header, however, does have a set of macros that allow a function with a variable argument list (such as printf) to be programmed in C.

All three printf family functions are of type int and return the number of characters actually written (in sprintf's case, they are written to an array). If an error occurs during output, printf and fprint return a negative value. No error is possible with sprintf.

The scanf Function

The scanf family (scanf, fscanf, and sscanf) are a series of crude functions that handle input from standard input, a file, or a string, respectively. While they can be quite useful for certain applications, their use for production data input can be messy and/or restrictive, as shall be shown. Unless otherwise stated, all references to scanf will include the scanf family.

Like printf, scanf uses an edit mask to determine the number and type of arguments to process and this mask may contain any combination of white-space, regular characters, and conversion-specifiers. The white-space may include only spaces, '\t' and '\n' characters, and causes all white-space in the input buffer to be skipped (from the current point). For example:

```
scanf(" %d ",&value);
```

---

causes all leading white-space to be ignored, then an `int` is read in and stored into value, then the next lot of white-space is skipped over. Any regular character (i.e., not white-space or part of a conversion specifier) must be matched exactly by an input character.

```
scanf("%d@",&count);
```

This example requires that a '@' character be input immediately following an int with no intervening white-space. If white-space is to be allowed, the mask should be "%d @" instead.

The format of a conversion specifier (or edit mask) is similar to that used by `printf`.

```
%[suppress][width][modifier]type
```

As shown, all parts except the leading % character and the trailing type specifier are optional.

A number of changes and enhancements have occurred regarding the `scanf` edit masks. The specifiers %e and %g are now synonyms for %f and they allow values with exponents containing either an 'e' or an 'E'. The letter 'h' could previously be used as a conversion type to indicate that a `short int` was expected. This must now be specified by using 'h' as a modifier along with one of the integer type letters 'd', 'i', 'o', 'u', or 'x'. 'h' is no longer a type.

The suppression character '*' can be used to skip over an input field. For example, a file may have been created by one program and parts of it need to be input to another program. The file has three int fields of widths 4, 5, and 6 characters, respectively and the second program needs only the first and third fields. The input format could be

```
int field1, field2;

scanf("%4d%*5d%6d ",&field1,&field3);
```

The specifier %*5d is a place holder and causes a 5-digit integer value to be input and discarded just so that scanf can position at the third field correctly, which it then inputs and stores in field3. The suppression character is of no use with scanf unless it is redirected to a file. There is no point soliciting user input and then discarding it.

The mask %i has been added to allow either decimal, octal, or hexadecimal input into the same field. For example, the format

```
scanf("%i",&value);
```

will accept any of the inputs 1234, 01377, and 0x3ff. Previously, the %d, %o, and %x masks were required to input values of their respective bases. Now all three can be handled by %i.

The mask %u has been added to allow unsigned input to be entered and the %p mask can be used to input a pointer value that was previously written out using printf with the mask %p. The format of a pointer display is implementation-defined. Since the addresses of objects can vary significantly from one program execution to the next, their values should not be saved across program executions. If you wish to get a reliable value when using %p on input, that pointer value must have been written out by the same program earlier in this execution. The argument corresponding to the %p mask must be a pointer to a pointer to void, *not* just a pointer to void.

The %n input mask is the converse of the %n mask used in printf. Here, it is used to record the number of characters read from the input stream thus far during the current call to scanf.

```
char *name;
int lenstr, value;

scanf("%s%n%d\n",name,&lenstr,&value);
```

Here, the length of the string read into name is stored in `lenstr`. While a trailing `'\0'` is appended to name, this is not included in the count.

The mask `%s` allows input strings to be processed, but it cannot handle strings with leading, embedded, or trailing spaces. For example, the conversion specifier

```
scanf("%s",&name);
```

will only store "The" when "The C Language" is entered. The input scan terminates at the first occurrence of white-space, that between "The" and "C". Instead, `%nc` could be used to read a string into a char array where n is the field width. But a problem occurs if the input string is not exactly n characters long because `%c` does not recognize white-space, it just reads exactly n characters no matter what they are. (With `%c`, the programmer must explicitly add the terminating `'\0'` if the array is to be treated as a string, while this is automatically done by `%s`.)

When dealing with interactive input from users, it is necessary to set both a maximum field width and the ability to stop scanning when white-space (or some other separator) is detected, and this combination is difficult (if not impossible) to achieve if input strings could legitimately contain white-space. The new mask `%[` may be be of some help. Its format is `%[ ... ]` where the ellipses represent a set of one or more characters that are used to control the input scan. If the first character in the brackets is `^`(a circumflex), then the scan for the input string terminates when an input character is found that matches any of the characters in the brackets (excluding the leading `^`). If a leading `^` is not present, the scan terminates at the first character that is not in the defined set. So to input a string with embedded spaces use

```
scanf("%[^\t\n]",string);
```

This would allow embedded spaces but not horizontal tabs or new lines. By using a maximum width, the scan can be terminated either on that many characters being input or by a tab or `newline` being entered. However, this does not allow less than the maximum width to be entered unless a tab or `newline` cause premature termination of the scan, and to achieve this, a character (for example a comma) needs to be reserved and placed it in the mask too, so that it could be used explicitly to end such a string.

Any white-space characters present in the `scanf` edit string cause white-space on input to be skipped, so care should be taken when leading white-space is actually part of an input string and must be preserved. Provided an input string is the last (or only) field to be input, then it can be easily handled using a mask of "...%[^\n]". In all other cases, the handling of these input strings can be quite messy.

Languages like FORTRAN and BASIC allow input arguments to be separated by commas with strings being quoted so they can include white-space and even commas. `scanf` does not directly support this method but it can be implemented with the appropriate mask. For example, the mask

```
scanf("%30[^,\n] ,%d",name,&value);
```

allows a string (possibly with embedded spaces) to be entered, followed by a comma, then by an integer. Either a 30-character string will be input or scanning for that string will stop when a comma or `newline` is entered. Then any white-space is skipped, the comma entered is matched and the `int` is processed. Note that if the %[scan is terminated by a comma, that comma remains in the input buffer and can be matched with the comma on the next scan.

This method does not allow commas in strings, however, but it is possible to allow strings to be entered if they are preceded and followed by some predictable character such as a double quote.

```
scanf("%*[^\"]%*c%[^\"]%*c",string);
```

Here, everything is skipped until the first quote is found, then that character is skipped and all subsequent characters up until the next quote are stored in string and finally the trailing quote is skipped. This method allows any embedded white-space (even across multiple input records) but it doesn't allow any embedded quotes. So it's still not a completely general solution.

Languages that allow input fields to be separated by commas often allow a null value by having two consecutive commas, possibly with some white-space between them. For example, FORTRAN allows an input line of "123,,456" when three integers are expected. The second integer defaults to zero. Similarly, a null argument for a string results in an empty string. This capability is not supported by scanf because the notion of field separators does not exist and is entirely user-definable.

The width specifier is a maximum value and problems can arise when it is used with the integral input mask %i. This mask allows decimal, octal, or hexadecimal values to be entered. Therefore, any width specified must take into account the leading "0" or "0x" that may be present.

The new data type long double has been added to the language, so the 'L' modifier has been added for use with %e, %f and %g. Note that a modifier of 'l' with these types is still required for double input, as without this modifier, float input is expected.

A specifier of %% requires that the next input character be a percent symbol. This mask is treated just like any non-white-space, non-mask character. If a lower-case conversion character other than 'c', 'd', 'e', 'f', 'g', 'i', 'n', 'o', 'p', 's', 'u', or 'x' is used, the behavior is undefined. If any other conversion character (except 'E', 'G', or 'X') is used the effects are implementation-defined. Lower-case conversion characters not currently used by the Standard are reserved for future use.

The three upper-case conversion characters listed above behave exactly the same as their lower-case counterparts and they are present purely for compatibility with their existence in printf (where they do have slightly different meanings).

Any input characters not used by scanf (including those which cause any conversion to terminate) are left in the input buffer and are available for use by the next input operation (which may be with scanf, getc, gets, etc.). Calls to the various character input functions can be interspersed without any problems, although the programmer must take care of flushing leading and/or trailing white-space before and after each call as necessary. scanf has no concept of input records, so it does not flush the input buffer between reads. It allows full type ahead (up the size of the stream's input buffer).

Some languages (most notably, BASIC) have an Input-with-Prompt capability where an input prompt message can be displayed as part of the input operation. This capability is not supported by scanf; it requires a separate (and previous) write using something like puts or printf.

Strangely, scanf and fscanf have no provision to report errors other than those pertaining to conversion. Errors are treated as end-of-file.

If scanf detects end-of-file in the middle of a conversion, that conversion terminates. If end-of-file is detected before the first mask conflict or conversion, then EOF is returned. If EOF is not detected, then the return value is the number of input values correctly assigned. This number does *not* include fields skipped over with the suppression character '*' or input characters that exactly matched characters in the edit mask. The success or failure of these two types of input can only be detected using the %n mask (making the comma-separator approach shown earlier even more messy).

To see if all desired input assignments took place, scanf's return value must be compared against the number possible. Even if the numbers match, this may not mean that all is well. Depending on the user mask and the user input, the values may match even though the input data was erroneous. Consider the mask "%lf %s" and the user input "1.23f03 FRED". The exponent inadvertently contains an 'f' instead of an 'e' (or 'E'), so the scan for the double value stops at the 'f'. No white-space is present in the input buffer, so the string is assigned the value "f03" and the trailing text "FRED" is left in the input buffer. The return value is 2, which is the number of assignments expected, so the program assumes all is well, but obviously it isn't. The problem is compounded further when the next input scan thinks it is dealing with new input when in fact it gets " FRED", which will most likely cause a conversion error. Obviously, an error may be detected some time after it has occurred by which time all association with the offending input may be lost.

It is also possible that if four input assignments are expected (for example) and only three occur, that the fourth input field is not the one in error. Depending on the input data and the format expected, it may have been any one of the first, second, or third, in which case the program must ask for the whole lot again; it may not be sufficient to just request that field that `scanf` presumably failed on.

The problems possible with `scanf` when inputting multiple fields per call have been shown and all of them point to the fact that if `scanf` is to be used at all, perhaps it should be limited to one field per call, as this would solve the field separator and embedded space requirements and the return value ambiguities. Despite its limitations, `scanf` can be quite useful in prototyping and writing programmer utilities where the user is well aware of `scanf`'s weaknesses and knows enough not to break it with strange or difficult input.

`stdio.h` **Revisited**

The `printf` and `scanf` family functions are quite large, because they have to be able to handle every possible format of I/O included in their definitions. Normally, with a linker there is no way to selectively include their support routines even though most programs won't use them. Some implementers supply two versions of these functions, one with full capabilities and one stripped-down (for example, without floating-point support) possibly called `_printf` and `_scanf`.

On floppy disk-based systems or systems with small amounts of memory (including ROM-based applications), the size of executable modules may be of considerable interest. This may also be true on fixed-memory operating systems where overlaying is either not possible or undesirable. For these (or other reasons), you may not want to use these functions.

One particular place where `printf` and `scanf` should not be used is in third-party or general-purpose libraries that are either sold or used for multiple applications. If a function in such a library uses `printf`, then no matter how much care the programmer takes to reduce the size of her program, she still gets large amounts of unused code loaded because of the application library routine she calls. Let the programmer decide for which big functions she wants to pay the price and use a simple set of string and formatted numeric functions instead.

There are a number of get/put functions that perform character and string I/O to files or standard devices and their differences can be quite confusing. For example, `gets` reads a string from `stdin` and discards any trailing `newline`, yet `fgets` (which reads from a file) retains a trailing `newline`. Conversely, `puts` appends a `newline` while `fputs` does not.

The macro FILE is often a structure that contains information about the current state of an open stream. Included in this information is error and end-of-file status. If the get routines detect EOF, they return this value and set the EOF flag in the stream's FILE structure. Likewise, if they detect an error, the error flag is set. These error and end-of-file states can be tested at any time, using the ferror and feof functions, respectively. The clearerr function can be used to clear these states. (Normally, these states are only cleared when a file is opened or the rewind function is used.)

Earlier in the discussion of math.h different methods of setting up a general-purpose error handler for domain and range errors were discussed. A similar general-purpose handler for I/O would also be useful. Implementing such a mechanism is no mean feat because there are considerable problems. First, not all functions report errors. Most of the input functions actually return EOF on error, which isn't particularly helpful if you need to recover in a meaningful way.

Whereas most of the math functions returns a double value, the I/O functions have different return types. Some return pointers to FILE where a NULL pointer implies an error, while others return an int where EOF means just that or possibly an error. Functions such as remove and rename return an int where a nonzero value indicates failure and the possible cause for failure is implementation-defined (and could possibly vary between remove and rename). Still other functions are type void and have no return value at all.

There is no simple way to pass off the return value from an I/O function to a general-purpose error processing function. The functions have to be broken into classes by return type and for those that can't distinguish between EOF and error, the ferror and feof functions must be used to determine the real return state.

Some of the I/O functions interface closely with the underlying file system. These include remove, rename, fopen, and fclose. The reasons for an error may involve any number of environmental problems such as "invalid file specification," "no such file or directory," and "insufficient access permission." For remove and rename, the nonzero error codes returned have implementation-defined meanings, as does fclose, but in the latter's case, it also considers an attempt to close a closed file to be an error. The fopen function, on the other hand, can only return a NULL pointer if an error occurs. It has no means of indicating what the problem was unless the error field in the FILE structure contains more than just a flag (such as an error code).

Apart from handling the myriad implementation-dependent errors possible, the Standard I/O mechanisms can only handle the simplest of file organizations: sequential text or binary in read, write, update, and append modes. Because of the many different random and indexed file systems in existence, no standard interface is workable. These capabilities must either be added as extensions to the existing library functions such as `fopen` or a separate set of implementation-defined I/O functions must be supplied. If the latter approach is used then the implementer has the ability to design them in such a way that error detection and handling is much more uniform than exists with the Standard I/O functions. Regardless of the method an implementer chooses to provide these extra capabilities, they must provide the functions exactly as they are defined in the Standard if they wish to conform.

A common requirement with interactive applications is that of data entry. While some of the I/O library functions in this area look attractive at first, they really aren't. Consider the case in which a background screen is to be painted and the user must enter fields left to right and top to bottom, and fields are validated on a field or character basis. The `scanf` functions have plenty of limitations, as mentioned earlier. Even though a maximum width can be specified, that only controls the number of characters scanned; it doesn't dictate the number that the user can actually enter. Even though a field width of 6 is used, there is nothing to stop the user entering 20, thus overwriting the background display. `scanf` will dutifully take the first 6 characters and if they are of the expected format, it will leave the excess characters in the input buffer for the next field (which is at a different place on the screen). The `gets` functions have no width specifier at all.

One common approach to data entry is to validate at the character level so that the user is informed immediately when an invalid response has been entered. Special cursor control keys or function keys are often supported to let the user back up or skip over input fields, and this requires that these special keys be recognized in any input field and handled specially. They are not invalid characters for a field and they should not cause any characters(s) to be echoed (unless this is specifically programmed into the system). This approach requires that characters be read with no echo. When a character is input, it should not automatically be echoed back to the terminal. It should be displayed there under program control when it is determined to be a nonspecial key. The problem here is that all of the library input routines that read from `stdin` echo their input and so can't be used for this purpose.

Another limitation of `scanf` and the `atof`, `atoi`, and `atol` functions declared in `stdlib.h` is that they stop converting an input value as soon as they detect an invalid character, in which case a numeric input field of "123d" would return the value 123 without error. If these functions are to be used, the length of the value returned must be compared with the length of the maximum possible value and, of course, one must take into account that "123" is valid. Just the fact that less than the maximum number has been entered is insufficient evidence to flag an input error, and these problems give more support to the single character input with the no-echo approach suggested above.

stdlib.h

Some of the limitations of the string conversion functions atoi, atol, and atof were discussed above. If they encounter an input value that cannot be represented (e.g., 40000 as input to a 16-bit signed int), the behavior is undefined (not implementation-defined) so error checking is impossible.

The functions strtod and strtol are more sophisticated versions of atof and atol, respectively. These functions terminate when the first unrecognized character is found and a pointer to this character can be returned. Underflow and overflow errors are recorded in errno. strtol converts a string to long int according to a base argument. If base is zero, input digits are assumed to be decimal unless a leading "0" or "0x" is present, in which case they are interpreted as octal and hexadecimal digits, respectively. Base may be in the range 2 to 36 where bases above 9 are represented by letters. One consequence of this is that binary values can be input as well.

The exit and onexit functions were discussed in detail in Chapter 9. The system function allows a string to be passed to the host command-line processor. The memory management functions calloc, malloc, realloc, and free were discussed earlier in this chapter with regard to pointer to void. They are also covered in Chapter 7.

string.h

Many of the string manipulation function names have the prefix str or mem, so to allow for future expansion of the library, identifiers with these prefixes are reserved. Some of these functions now accept and return pointer to void arguments and these were discussed earlier in this chapter. If any string copy function involves the copying of overlapping strings, the results are undefined.

The format for using strncpy is

```
char *strncpy(char *s1, const char *s2, size_t n);
```

If the string pointed to by s2 is shorter than n characters, then extra '\0' characters are appended until n characters have been written in total. If the string pointed to by s2 is longer than n, then the string s1 may not be terminated with a '\0'. On the other hand, strncat always terminates the string with a '\0'.

Some implementations have the string comparison functions return -1, 0, or +1 to indicate less than, equal and greater than, respectively. These numeric values are special cases and are not universally used. The Standard only requires that the corresponding return values be negative, zero, and positive. If one of the characters being compared has its high-order bit set, the sign of the result is implementation-defined.

The strchr function locates the first occurrence of a character in a string, while strrchr finds the last such occurrence.

```
char *strchr(const char *s, int c);
char *strrchr(const char *s, int c);
```

In both functions, the '\0' terminating the string being searched *is* considered to be part of the string. This means that the character being searched for could be '\0'. Since this character, by definition, can only exist at the end of the string, this nonstandard approach seems odd. In such a search, both functions will return a pointer to the terminating '\0', which could just as well have been found by using strlen. These are the only instances in C where the trailing '\0' is considered to be part of a string.

Character arrays are often used to store strings, but they don't have to be. For example, many terminals and special devices recognize escape sequences that can be used to switch display modes, graphics, and plot modes, etc., and these sequences can be stored in char arrays. Frequently, all 8 bits of a byte are needed to implement some of these sequences. In fact, a char with a value of zero may even be used to reset certain display modes, and such a character may be confused with a string terminator if the str* and mem* functions are used. These functions should be used with care when dealing with nonstring char arrays.

Strings can be of any length and are typically terminated by a '\0'. While this definition allows a simple, yet powerful set of library functions to be defined, it does require that the whole string be scanned in order to find its length. Other languages prepend a string descriptor to each string which contains the current length of that string and this method can be applied to C programs. Provided you don't use library functions that depend on a terminating '\0', there is absolutely no requirement to have one.

Consider a full-screen editor or text processing program that is constantly dealing with strings whose lengths may vary at any time. In this case it would be far too time-consuming to scan each string to find its length each time it changes. More likely, string lengths will be stored as part of, or separately from, the string, as follows:

```
struct str {
    int length;
    char *string;
} strings[100];
```

Here, each element in the strings array contains a string length and a pointer to the beginning of the string. If the element is unused, the pointer is NULL. (Note that a length of 0 cannot be used to indicate that a null string has length zero. Perhaps a value of -1 could be used as an available-slot flag.) Since the length of each string is known, strings can be copied and compared using strncpy and strncmp even though no terminating '\0' characters exist.

In Chapter 1 the copying and comparing of structures was discussed in detail. Generally, the string functions are inadequate for these tasks as structures can legitimately have embedded binary zero char values and these would cause premature termination on copying or comparisons.

The ANSI Standard Headers

The information in this appendix is taken from the proposed ANSI Standard draft, dated November 1985. While most of these headers will likely remain the same in the final Standard, they are subject to change. New headers and/or identifiers may be added (and therefore will become reserved) and identifiers may be removed or have their name changed. Note that the identifier lists include both macro and function names.

The reader is referred to the official Standard Documents for a precise definition of the standard header contents.

The proposed Standard headers and their purpose are as follows.

Header	Purpose
assert.h	program diagnostic purposes
ctype.h	character testing & conversion
float.h	floating type characteristics
limits.h	integral type sizes
math.h	math functions
setjmp.h	nonlocal jump facility
signal.h	signal handling
stdarg.h	variable argument support
stddef.h	miscellaneous
stdio.h	input/output functions
stdlib.h	general utilities
string.h	string functions
time.h	date and time functions

The following list contains the header identifiers in alphabetical order within header.

Header	Identifier
assert.h	assert
	NDEBUG
ctype.h	isalnum
	isalpha
	iscntrl
	isdigit
	isgraph
	islower
	isprint
	ispunct
	isspace
	isupper
	isxdigit
	tolower
	toupper

float.h and limits.h contain many more macro definitions. The complete list has yet to be finalized.

Header	Identifier
math.h	acos
	asin
	atan2
	atan
	ceil
	cosh
	cos
	EDOM
	ERANGE
	exp
	fabs
	floor

Header	Identifier
math.h (cont)	fmod
	frexp
	HUGE_VAL
	idiv
	idiv_t
	ldiv
	ldiv_t
	ldexp
	log10
	log
	modf
	pow
	sinh
	sin
	sqrt
	tanh
	tan
setjmp.h	jmp_buf
	longjmp
	setjmp
signal.h	kill
	SIGABRT
	SIGFPE
	SIGILL
	SIGINT
	signal
	SIGSEGV
	SIGTERM
	SIG_DFL
	SIG_ERR
	SIG_IGN
stdarg.h	va_arg
	va_end
	va_list
	va_start
stddef.h	errno
	NULL
	ptrdiff_t
	size_t

Header	Identifier
stdio.h	BUFSIZ
	clearerr
	EOF
	fclose
	feof
	ferror
	fflush
	fgetc
	fgets
	FILE
	fopen
	fprintf
	fputc
	fputs
	fread
	freopen
	fscanf
	fseek
	ftell
	fwrite
	getchar
	getc
	gets
	L_tmpnam
	perror
	printf
	putchar
	putc
	puts
	remove
	rename
	rewind
	scanf
	SEEK_CUR
	SEEK_END
	SEEK_SET
	setbuf
	setvbuf
	sprintf
	sscanf
	stderr
	stdin
	stdout

Header	Identifier
stdio.h (cont)	SYS_OPEN
	tmpfile
	tmpnam
	TMP_MAX
	ungetc
	vfprintf
	vprintf
	vsprintf
	_IOFBF
	_IOLBF
	_IONBF
stdlib.h	abort
	abs
	atof
	atoi
	atol
	calloc
	exit
	free
	getenv
	malloc
	onexit
	rand
	realloc
	srand
	strtod
	strtol
	system
string.h	memchr
	memcmp
	memcpy
	memset
	strcat
	strchr
	strcmp
	strcpy
	strcspn
	strerror
	strlen
	strncat
	strncmp

Header	Identifier
string.h (cont)	strncpy
	strpbrk
	strrchr
	strspn
	strstr
	strtok
time.h	asctime
	CLK_TCK
	clock
	clock_t
	ctime
	difftime
	gmtime
	localtime
	time
	time_t
	tm
predefined	__DATE__
macros	__FILE__
	__LINE__
	__TIME__

The following list contains all header identifiers in alphabetical order. This list may be used as the basis for a project's reserved identifier list. (float.h and limits.h contain many more macro definitions. The complete list has yet to be finalized.)

Identifier	Header	
__DATE__	predefined	macro
__FILE__	"	"
__LINE__	"	"
__TIME__	"	"
_IOFBF	stdio.h	
_IOLBF	stdio.h	
_IONBF	stdio.h	
abort	stdlib.h	
abs	stdlib.h	

Identifier	Header
acos	math.h
asctime	time.h
asin	math.h
assert	assert.h
atan2	math.h
atan	math.h
atof	stdlib.h
atoi	stdlib.h
atol	stdlib.h
BUFSIZ	stdio.h
calloc	stdlib.h
ceil	math.h
clearerr	stdio.h
CLK_TCK	time.h
clock	time.h
clock_t	time.h
cosh	math.h
cos	math.h
ctime	time.h
difftime	time.h
EDOM	math.h
EOF	stdio.h
ERANGE	math.h
errno	stddef.h
exit	stdlib.h
exp	math.h
fabs	math.h
fclose	stdio.h
feof	stdio.h
ferror	stdio.h
fflush	stdio.h
fgetc	stdio.h
fgets	stdio.h
FILE	stdio.h
floor	math.h
fmod	math.h
fopen	stdio.h
fprintf	stdio.h
fputc	stdio.h
fputs	stdio.h
fread	stdio.h
free	stdlib.h
freopen	stdio.h

Identifier	Header
frexp	math.h
fscanf	stdio.h
fseek	stdio.h
ftell	stdio.h
fwrite	stdio.h
getchar	stdio.h
getc	stdio.h
getenv	stdlib.h
gets	stdio.h
gmtime	time.h
HUGE_VAL	math.h
idiv	math.h
idiv_t	math.h
isalnum	ctype.h
isalpha	ctype.h
iscntrl	ctype.h
isdigit	ctype.h
isgraph	ctype.h
islower	ctype.h
isprint	ctype.h
ispunct	ctype.h
isspace	ctype.h
isupper	ctype.h
isxdigit	ctype.h
jmp_buf	setjmp.h
kill	signal.h
ldexp	math.h
ldiv	math.h
ldiv_t	math.h
localtime	time.h
log10	math.h
log	math.h
longjmp	setjmp.h
L_tmpnam	stdio.h
malloc	stdlib.h
memchr	string.h
memcmp	string.h
memcpy	string.h
memset	ptrdiff_t
modf	math.h
NDEBUG	assert.h
NULL	stddef.h
onexit	stdlib.h

Identifier	Header
perror	stdio.h
pow	math.h
printf	stdio.h
ptrdiff_t	stddef.h
putchar	stdio.h
putc	stdio.h
puts	stdio.h
rand	stdlib.h
realloc	stdlib.h
remove	stdio.h
rename	stdio.h
rewind	stdio.h
scanf	stdio.h
SEEK_CUR	stdio.h
SEEK_END	stdio.h
SEEK_SET	stdio.h
setbuf	stdio.h
setjmp	setjmp.h
setvbuf	stdio.h
SIGABRT	signal.h
SIGFPE	signal.h
SIGILL	signal.h
SIGINT	signal.h
signal	signal.h
SIGSEGV	signal.h
SIGTERM	signal.h
SIG_DFL	signal.h
SIG_ERR	signal.h
SIG_IGN	signal.h
sinh	math.h
sin	math.h
size_t	stddef.h
sprintf	stdio.h
sqrt	math.h
srand	stdlib.h
sscanf	stdio.h
stderr	stdio.h
stdin	stdio.h
stdout	stdio.h
strcat	string.h
strchr	string.h
strcmp	string.h
strcpy	string.h

Identifier	Header
strcspn	string.h
strerror	string.h
strlen	string.h
strncat	string.h
strncmp	string.h
strncpy	string.h
strpbrk	string.h
strrchr	string.h
strspn	string.h
strstr	string.h
strtod	stdlib.h
strtok	string.h
strtol	stdlib.h
system	stdlib.h
SYS_OPEN	stdio.h
tanh	math.h
tan	math.h
time	time.h
time_t	time.h
tmpfile	stdio.h
tmpnam	stdio.h
TMP_MAX	stdio.h
tm	time.h
tolower	ctype.h
toupper	ctype.h
ungetc	stdio.h
va_arg	stdarg.h
va_end	stdarg.h
va_list	stdarg.h
va_start	stdarg.h
vfprintf	stdio.h
vprintf	stdio.h
vsprintf	stdio.h

APPENDIX B

Information on the ANSI Standard

The ANSI X3J11 Committee expects to release a draft Standard for public comment after their June, 1986 meeting. Comments will then be accepted. Each comment will receive a formal, written response. After that review period expires, all necessary changes will be made and the draft will be released for a second review after which time it will be voted on by full Committee (and the X3 Secretariat) before becoming an official ANSI Standard. This whole process may be completed by mid-1987 but since much of the current draft Standard is unlikely to change, implementers are already beginning to provide many of the new capabilities. Microsoft's V3.0 MS-DOS compiler and the latest compilers from MetaWare are such examples. Obviously, until there is an official Standard, implementations cannot claim Standard conformance.

The aims of the Standard are:

1. To preserve the spirit of C as a sparse language and to not unduly add to the language, but rather to define and consolidate it, removing all known ambiguities in the definition, particularly in the library.

2. To break as little existing code as possible except where existing practices directly contradict a reasonable, consolidated approach. If code is to be broken, it must be done in such a way that the results are obviously wrong, by way of translation diagnostics and/or obvious run-time errors.

3. To add new capabilities that directly add functionality or provide assistance in writing "better" programs. Examples of these are the addition of function prototypes and the variable type modifiers const and volatile.

4. To add capabilities that assist in program portability. Included in this category is the stdarg header, which provides a mechanism for using variable argument lists in a portable fashion.

Copies of the (draft) Standard and the accompanying Rationale Document are available from

```
X3 Secretariat CBEMA
311 First Street, NW
Suite 500
Washington, D.C. 20001
(202) 737-8888
```

For more information about the X3J11 Committee's activities, contact:

```
Dr. Thomas Plum
X3J11 Vice Chair
Plum Hall, Inc.
1 Spruce Ave
Cardiff, NJ 08232
(609) 927-3770
```

Regular information about the Committee's activities is reported in

```
Rex Jaeschke's column in

The Programmer's Journal
Oakley Publishing Company
P.O. Box 30160
Eugene, OR 97403.
```

and

```
Tom Plum's Column in
The C Journal
InfoPro Systems
3108 Route 10
Denville, NJ 07834
(201) 989-0570
```

Public and on-site seminars covering the impact of the proposed ANSI Standard are available from

---

```
Rex Jaeschke
2051 Swans Neck Way
Reston, VA 22091
(703) 860-0091

Other seminars available include:
    - The truth about C
    - Introductory C
    - Advanced C
    - Writing Portable Programs in C
    - C and efficiency

Consulting services available include
    - Evaluating the suitability of C for projects
    - Selection of C language development tools
    - Defining a debugging strategy
    - Establishing documentation and programming standards
    - Recommendation of quality assurance procedures
```

APPENDIX C

Recommended Reading

The Following texts are recommended for further reading.

"The (draft) ANSI C Language Standard" and the accompanying "Rationale Document." The Standard defines the preprocessor, language, and library, and except for a few notes and examples, it makes no attempt to explain how a particular part of C should or could be used. It is a Standard definition, not a C tutorial. The Rationale Document is not part of the Standard but it attempts to explain some of the rationale used in making decisions in the X3J11 Committee. This document plays an important role in helping to interpret the more formal Standard. It also indicates those circumstances where programs processed by conforming translators will not break in obvious ways, but rather will behave differently in "quiet" ways. Refer to Appendix B for more information on the Standard.

Harbison, Samuel P. and Guy L. Steele Jr. *A C Reference Manual* Prentice-Hall, Englewood Cliffs, NJ., 1984. ISBN: 0-13-110016-5 (hardcover), 0-13-110008-4 (paperback). This text has a style similar to that of K&R, but it reflects common (and more current) interpretations of C in different machine environments. Like K&R, this book is oriented more toward a formal definition of C, rather than showing the reader how to work with or solve problems in C.

Kernighan, Brian W. and Dennis M. Ritchie. *The C Programming Language,* Prentice-Hall, Englewood Cliffs, NJ. 1978. ISBN: 0-13-110163-3. This is the definitive C reference book and most implementation manuals refer to it. While somewhat outdated, it remains a valuable reference book.

MetaWare, Inc. *MetaWare C Language Reference Manual* 412 Liberty Street, Santa Cruz, CA 95060: (Telephone (408) 429-META). This manual is a terse, formal, and precise definition of the C language that is recommended for rigorous research and use by implementers.

CROSS-REFERENCE INDEX

249

X3J11 (*continued*)
    stderr, buffering of, 193
    str prefix, 167
    strchr, 231
    strcspn, 197
    strrchr, 231
    strspn, 197
    strtod, 230
    strtol, 230
    structures, arguments of, 17, 82, 128
    structures, assignment of, 17
    structures, holes, location of, 16
    structures, namespace of, 16
    structures, return values, as, 17, 82

X3J11 (*continued*)
    system, 230
    SYS_OPEN, 194
    __TIME__, 164
    underscore, identifiers with leading, 164
    unions, arguments of, 44
    unions, assignment of, 17, 43
    unions, bit fields and, 28
    unions, initialization of, 45
    unions, namespace of, 43
    unions, return values of, 44
    void *, 73
    volatile, 200